SAILING MADE EASY

AND

COMFORT IN SMALL CRAFT

ALSO

HOW TO RUN A MOTOR CRUISER

Revised Edition 1930
Reprinted . . 1934
Reprinted . . 1937
Reprinted . . 1946
Reprinted . . 1948
Reprinted . . 1949
Reprinted . . 1951

SAILING MADE EASY

AND

COMFORT IN
SMALL CRAFT

ALSO

HOW TO RUN A MOTOR CRUISER

A PRACTICAL HANDBOOK OF
SAILING AND COOKERY

BY S. J. HOUSLEY

WITH DIAGRAMS

BLAKES (NORFOLK BROADS HOLIDAYS) LTD.
TEMPLE BAR HOUSE, 23/28 FLEET STREET
LONDON, E.C.4

MADE AND PRINTED IN GREAT BRITAIN
BY JARROLD AND SONS LTD. NORWICH

CONTENTS

SAILING MADE EASY
AND
COMFORT IN SMALL CRAFT

CHAPTER I

INTRODUCTORY

So much has been written justly about the delights of a holiday spent in sailing upon the Norfolk rivers and similar waters, that I need not add another voice to the chorus of enthusiasm. But I would draw attention to a point which has not received all the appreciation it deserves, to wit, that sailing in such waters provides the best training for a beginner that could well be devised.

I was recently confiding to a friend that I had written this little book on seamanship for beginners sailing on inland waters. "Not much seamanship needed, I should imagine," was his comment. Nothing could be farther from the truth; and yet the remark was not wholly without reason. For, although the sailor in narrow waters is called upon to

1

perform daily, hourly, and every two minutes
acts of seamanship which the sea-farer may
only have occasion to practise at rare intervals,
yet the penalties attaching to mistakes in
narrow waters are usually mild in comparison
with those exacted by the sea.

The rivers of Norfolk are a judicious
schoolmaster. They give the pupil plenty
of exercises, corrected by mild punishment
for mistakes due to inexperience. Indeed,
few can sail these waters without picking up
some new and useful wrinkle. " A stretch
off the land " is unknown here. The mind
must be awake and alert the whole time.
Almost every situation considered by the
" Rule of the Road " may here be met with
in the course of a single hour. Almost every
morning we have to make sail, and almost
every evening to stow it. Coming to an
anchor is a necessity at each meal. As the
rivers wind among the marshes, the shortest
passage will call for exercise on every point
of sailing, by, on and off the wind. To the
man who " can't be bothered," this is no doubt
a drawback. To the accomplished sailor it
is a delight. To the learner it offers invalu-
able opportunities.

It is as a help and an encouragement to the learner that I have written this little book. I have endeavoured to make it so simple as to be intelligible to the uninitiated and so thorough as to be of real, practical assistance. Comfort, the first word of the title, is the keynote; comfort material and moral, especially the latter. No one in his senses is indifferent to lack of food, warmth and shelter. But in regard to dangers of which we are unaware we can show an indifference astounding to those who have clearer vision.

May I be forgiven if I am doing an injustice, but I suspect, from observation, that the need of exhortation to good works on deck is greater than that of awakening the conscience in regard to things below. Wherefore, out of eight chapters, six and a half are devoted to the business of the skipper and his mate, one to the cook and a half to the cabin boy.

To point out that dinner has little interest for a drowned man would be to push truth to a brutal extreme. But most of us who have sailed much, will admit that supper is sweeter when you have not made an ass of yourself or are free from an uncomfortable suspicion that you may have done so.

There is a wise and ever-increasing company who spend their summer holiday afloat. If this little book succeed in adding to the safety, comfort or enjoyment of one of these, I shall be paid for my labour. Rome was not built in a day, nor is seamanship to be learned in a month. But let the novice tackle this book with patience, courage, and Chapter X., and all shall be well.

CHAPTER II

ON SETTING SAIL AND GETTING UNDER WAY

WE will suppose that your ship is moored alongside the rond with two rond anchors, one at the bow and one at the stern; that your awning and sail-cover are on and everything stowed as it should have been overnight —in fact that you are about to get under way, beginning at the very beginning.

A.—CLEARING FOR ACTION

I. *Furl the awning*. This may appear an unnecessary trouble, but:—A properly furled awning lasts longer, looks better and keeps its shape better than one which has been rolled up anyhow. It is easier to stow, it is *much easier to rig*. The moment you bring it on deck you can see "which way it goes." You don't find that you are getting it rigged

wrong end foremost or inside out and have
to begin again and reverse the whole thing,
perhaps after a hard day's work and the rain
just about to come down in buckets. You
don't have to haul fathom after fathom of
shapeless bundle out of your forepeak, because
you can't lower your mast till you have got
"that infernal thing" out of the way. You
will find it less trouble ultimately to furl the
awning properly than not to do it. So do
it. Thus :—

Cast off the points or lacings of the awning
except the one round the mast and the two
foremost ones. These will hold the forward
end of the awning from blowing about and
confusing your work while you are folding it
up. Bring the after end forward along the
boom about a yard and try to arrange that
the fold shall come on a seam. Fold the flaps
of the awning back on top of this fold, as flat
as possible. Take hold of the after edge of
the fold and fold again the same width as
before. Continue to fold till you come to
the mast. Cast off the lacing round the
mast and the two forward points. Fold back
the forward edge of the awning on to the
part already folded. Now take both bottom

edges of the folded awning and bring them up together to the boom. Halve these folds again up to the boom. Turn one half of the awning over the boom, folding it on to the other half. Your awning now lies on the cabin-top a nice flat parcel about three feet square. Stow it. (The forepeak is the usual place. It must be kept dry.) *Remove the spreaders*, which supported the awning over the well, and stow them. (The bottom of the dinghy is handy and out of the way.)

II. Fold up the sail - cover in a similar manner, from aft forward to the mast. Stow it in a dry place.

III. Take a look round below, to see that things are so stowed that they won't get adrift and possibly get smashed when the fun begins. Remember the things in the lockers.

IV. Lower the cabin-top, if of the " lifting " variety, and *see the canvas is not pinched*.

B.—Setting Sail

I. If you are on the windward shore, "get" your after anchor and let the ship swing head to wind to the forward anchor.

If you are on the lee shore, take a warp and

anchor across in the dinghy, or use the quant, and having "got" your anchors, go across to the windward shore and make fast with the forward anchor.   Under certain circumstances it may be possible, and desirable, to get under way from a lee shore.   But in nearly every case, ninety-nine in a hundred, it is best to go to the windward shore if you are not there to start with.

II. *Hook or shackle on the halyards*, taking care to see that the "leads" are right, *i.e.*, that the ropes go from block to block without crossing one another anywhere.   A "turn" in a halyard looks unsailorlike and chafes the rope. In the throat halyard or the jib halyard it may prevent your getting the sail up properly.

Make fast the end of the throat halyard, so that it cannot get out of reach or get foul of other rigging.

Set up the peak halyard just taut — not enough to lift the boom out of the crutches, but just enough to take the weight of the gaff—*and belay*.   If you omit this, the gaff will fall on the deck or the cabin-top when you cast off the peak tyer.   (Every bump knocks off a bit of value.)

III. *Overhaul the main-sheet* and see that

the "fall" is coiled so that it is "free for running." (Let the coil lie with the end at the bottom.) If you omit to overhaul the main-sheet you won't be able to "top the boom," and you will have two pulls at the topping-lift instead of one, the first pull having proved a "frost." (Hope nobody was looking!)

IV. *Top the boom* by hauling on the topping-lift till the boom just clears the crutches. *Belay.* Be careful about belaying this, because if the boom and sail fell on any one, by reason of the topping-lift giving way, there would be hard words and broken bones. (At all times stand from under the boom.) Do not top the boom too high and there will be no reason to alter the peak halyard again. But note that it is handy, as peak halyard and topping-lift are frequently working in concert, to have the pins or cleats, to which these are belayed, within easy hail of one another, next if possible.

While you top the boom, somebody must "stand by" the crutches, which otherwise may cause a loss of time by going overboard and having to be rescued. Crutches should, however, be secured against this by a piece of lacing (*vide* chap. vii.). Belay the main-sheet, but not hard down, just enough to control the boom. *Stow the crutches.* They will go well with the spreaders.

V. Lay *the jib* on the fore-deck. Shackle the tack of the jib to the stem-head. If your boat has a bowsprit, set up the bobstay, hook the tack of the jib to the "traveller," haul out and belay. (Most jibs are marked head and tack, whereby the sailor may avoid setting his jib wrong end up, in which position it is not so effective as it might be. But it is a safe rule to remember that *the luff-rope* of a jib *is on the port side of the sail,* as with almost all fore-and-aft sails. If you remember this, you cannot set your jib wrong end up.)

Shackle the jib-sheets to the clew, and see that they have no turns in them. Many boats now sailing the Broads are fitted with a jib having a boom and only one jib-sheet, one end of which is shackled to a ringbolt on the port side of the fore-deck. The other end is rove through a thimble eye on the boom of the jib—we cannot call this spar a jib-boom —then through a bull's eye on the starboard side of the deck, opposite the ringbolt, and then is led aft to the well.

Hook or shackle on the jib halyard, taking care that the leads are fair and that there are no turns in the luff rope of the jib. If the jib has been properly furled overnight there will be no difficulty, but if it has just been bundled up anyhow there may be trouble.

Just take a turn with the end of the jib halyard round its cleat or belaying pin, and at the same time catch in the head of the jib. This is to prevent the jib blowing overboard or the end of the halyard getting adrift or foul of something.

VI. Cast off the tyers or lacing from the mainsail, except the peak tyer. Most yachts in Norfolk lace up the mainsail and do not use tyers. But the peak should always have its own tyer or lacing. We are now ready to set sail.

VII. You will not have forgotten, of course, to coil all your tyers or lacings and stow them.

Cast off the peak tyer, coil and stow.

Man the peak halyard. Raise the peak until it shows *between* the topping-lifts. If there is only one topping - lift this will be unnecessary; but see that the sail goes up *its own side* of the lift.

2

Man the throat halyard. Hauling on this
and on the other simultaneously, let the sail
go up with the gaff at right angles to the
mast. When the throat is up, *belay the peak
halyard.* The luff of the sail is now "hand
taut." Set it up "bar taut"—as rigid as a
piece of iron—by swigging. (Few yachts on
the Broads are large enough to require a
"purchase" on the halyards, and a good
swig will set up the luff quite sufficiently.
A taut luff is necessary with every sail.)
Belay the throat halyard. Coil the fall so
that it is handy for letting go in case of
need. If you lay it on deck, lay it with the
end at the bottom, so that it is "free for
running." This should be done with all
halyards and ropes whatsoever. A coil laid
on deck, however, gets adrift or goes overboard or makes itself conspicuous in some
ingenious way; so it is best to stow it to
avoid trouble. It is fairly handy to nip part
of the coil in between the mast and the
standing part of the halyard. Only be careful
that no part of the coil projects foreside of
the mast or it will take hold of the end of
the boom of the jib, which might result in
your being set ashore.

Hoist the peak till a small "girt" appears in the throat in a direction upwards from the mast towards the gaff; not downwards from the throat towards the boom, which would indicate that your peak was too low. The girts which have been made in the right direction will mostly disappear when you let go your topping-lift and the weight of the boom comes on the sail, and will disappear finally as the peak settles down, which it is sure to do. A small remaining girt does not matter. Big girts show that your peak is too high, in which case you must ease up the peak halyard a few inches.

Belay, coil and stow the peak halyard.

VIII. See that the jib-sheets are so free that the jib when hoisted cannot exercise any influence on the position of your ship before you want it to, otherwise there may be trouble, especially if you are single-handed. The jib should flap about aimlessly while you are hoisting, not take charge of the ship. So let all sheets, or the one above described be slacked right off. Don't get in the way of the jib yourself. Hoist the jib and *get the luff bar taut.* If your boat has a bow-sprit, heave until the luff of the jib takes the weight of the mast and mainsail, until the forestay—which, in Norfolk, goes to the bowsprit end — hangs in a graceful bight inside the luff of the sail. The modern cruiser on the Broads usually has no bowsprit, or at most a bumpkin. A bowsprit is not a handy thing in narrow waters bordered by tall and strong reeds.

Belay, coil and stow.

IX. *Let go your topping-lift* and *overhaul,* so that the whole weight of the boom may come on the sail. Belay, coil and stow.

X. Stow your warps and after rond anchor where they will not get adrift and cause annoyance, but *you should always have them in a handy place* in case they are wanted in a hurry The cabin floor is safe and easily accessible, if the presence of warps there is not too inconvenient.

I remember coming through Ludham Bridge one day, going up-stream, with a very strong N.E. wind blowing across the river. Just above the bridge is a patch of clay into which my quant stuck, so that by no means could I get it out, and I had to let go. A crowd of yachts lay on the lee shore. (Why so many people seem to prefer the lee shore, I never

can make out.) We were now in serious
danger of being blown across the river foul
of some of these craft. Calling to my friend
on the helm to head her towards the windward bank, I made a warp fast to a cleat on
the ship's head, took the warp in the dinghy,
pulled ashore with it and got the ship tied
up in safety. All this had to be done in
less time than it takes to write it, and would
not have been done had the warp been stowed
in some inaccessible spot with a pile of stuff
on top of it.

Always have a warp and an anchor handy.
It is the unexpected which always happens,
and the true sailorman is always ready for it.

XI. See that everything you have in the
dinghy is properly stowed—crutches, spreaders,
mop, oars, mast and sails if she have them—
and that nothing, with the possible exception
of the mast, projects above her gunwales.
Her own crutches, rowlocks or tholes must
be removed. Projections on dinghys are
frequent causes of mishap. Make the dinghy
fast to the yacht on a *short* towline. It is
very annoying, when turning to windward
in a narrow passage, to find that your dinghy
has sailed at the end of a nice long line among

the reeds, and anchored you securely by the stern, just as you are paying off to make the next board.   So *keep the dinghy close up.*

You are now ready to get your forward anchor.

C.—Shoving off

When the wind is in the sails, the mainsail has a tendency—a very strong tendency—to swing the ship round head to wind.   The jib, being foreside of the mast, exercises an influence in the other direction.   It tends to pull the vessel's head away from the wind, to cause her to "pay off."   In a boat whose sails are properly balanced, the combined tendency is in favour of the mainsail.   The ship *always* has a tendency to "fly up in the wind."   This tendency is corrected by the helm, which, while the ship is keeping a straight course, will have to be "aweather" —a little bit "up" to windward more or less according to the sail set and the amount of the wind.   But the helm has no effect upon a vessel which is not "under way," which has not "steerage way" on.

Suppose, for illustration, that you were lying

with the wind abeam and your sails empty and flapping. If you haul down the main-sheet and fill the mainsail the ship's head will at once go to windward, the mainsail exercising its influence while the jib does nothing. If, on the other hand, you leave the main-sheet loose and haul aft the jib-sheet, so as to fill the jib, then the jib will at once pull her head off to leeward.

Suppose you are head to wind, the mainsail being then necessarily empty, by pulling either jib-sheet or holding the jib out on either side by hand, you make a *backsail* of it and cause it, while giving her slight "stern-way," to pay her head off on the opposite side. That is common-sense. Think of it. Head to wind. Haul aft your port jib-sheet. The wind catching on the back of the sail so held over to port causes her head to go to starboard, and *vice versa*. That is "paying her head off."

Now to shove off. We have been a long time coming to it, but we must get things right; and there are two great truths which I would impress upon all that go down to the sea in sail. They are:—(1) "Time does not matter;" (2) "It is better to be sure than sorry."

Let us take two leading cases. You are in the windward bank.

I. Wind at right angles to bank, blowing straight across the stream. Your ship will lie in the same direction head to wind and across the stream. Go ashore and get your anchor; and stow it in such a way that it can't slip overboard accidentally and anchor you when you are under way and would rather it did not. As you come aboard, give her head a shove towards the direction in which you propose to proceed. Either by hand or by means of the sheet, keep your jib aweather to pay her off. *Don't be in a hurry to fill your mainsail* or she may "fly in the wind" and run into the bank. As soon as she is well clear of the bank, let draw your jib, *i.e.*, trim the sheet as you will have it for sailing (*vide* chap. iii. p. 22), and *when she has steerageway*, trim your mainsail and sail her.

You may find that you have to use the quant to shove her head off in the first instance. I also assume that you have a friend standing by the helm. If you have not, you must get her head off with the jib, as advised, and quant if necessary, having been extra careful to have your main-sheet overhauled, and make a dash for the helm as soon as she has paid off enough.

II. Wind at such an angle that it is much easier to get under way one way than the other. The easier is, of course, the right way, to windward. I have seen people try the other. Then the mainsail fills before she has way and before her head is sufficiently off, and bump she goes into the bank again! I have seen a boat go quite a long way like this, in a series of hops. It is not good for the boat and very unhealthy for other craft moored in the vicinity. Don't do it so, but :—

Get under way to windward, as above, case I. If you wish to proceed to windward, you do so. But if you wish to proceed to leeward, you still get under way to windward ; because it is much easier to turn the ship round when the bank is not in the light. Thus, being under way to windward, make a " board " across the river. Put the helm *hard* down. When she is past the position of head to wind, keep the jib-sheet aweather to pay her head off; or, if you have a single sheet, send the crew forward to hold the boom of the jib aweather. The helm that was hard "down" has now become, by virtue of the ship's change of position, hard "up." Keep it so. *Overhaul* the main-sheet ; for, if the mainsail were to fill now, she might refuse to pay off and you would go into the bank. As soon as she is right round and on her course, trim your sails, ease your helm and sail her.

If the wind were blowing along the bank and you wished to proceed to leeward, you might be able to swing her off the wind at the start and proceed to leeward at once. But the manœuvre is not recommended. *Get under way to windward.* Let this be your standard rule. Then if you want to proceed to leeward, make a board and swing her round. If you *have* to get under way from a lee-shore, you are in an undesirable position. You may find it an impossibility. You will certainly find setting sail an awkward job. Taking advantage of stream or tide, making good use of your experience and the quant, you may succeed.

But you should not have anchored in such a position as to be reduced to these desperate expedients. Always, when anchoring, think of the morrow's start. Pick your anchorage, so that from whatever direction the wind may blow, there is some handy spot near from which to make your start. If the worst come to the worst, and you find that you cannot get under way from where you are, then use the quant and shove her till you have reached some place from which you can get away.

Stream and tide will modify the conditions described in cases I. and II. But you will find it simple enough in practice if you follow the rule of always making your first "cast" in the easiest direction and swinging your ship round afterwards if necessary by the manœuvre described above. In fact, the ability to execute that evolution with ease is the key to the difficulty of getting under way. Study it.

CHAPTER III

[*N.B.*—I recommend the novice reading this
chapter (and others, but especially this
one and chap. v.) to make free use of
diagrams with pencil and paper.]

A.—REACHING

You have got under way in the circumstances of case I. in the preceding chapter,
p. 18 ; the wind is abeam and you are on
starboard tack, *i.e.*, the wind is coming from
your starboard hand. Give all your sails as
much sheet as you can without letting them
shake in the luff. When they shake in the
luff they are telling you that they have not
got all the wind they want, and you must
haul your sheets a bit till the sails "draw."
You keep a slight pressure on the helm, "up,"

22

to counteract the boat's tendency to go to windward.

Don't go too near the windward bank. A sudden puff of wind might cause her to fly into the windward bank before you could stop her with the helm, and sudden puffs are by no means rare in river sailing.

B.—Running

The next reach of the river bears away to the left. Keeping the helm up, steer her past the corner (see note at the end of the chapter on steering). You will now find that she wants more sheet. Give it her, or you will not be doing as well as you should. The ruffle of the water under the lee is a fair guide for the mainsail. Let the boom be about parallel to the wavelets.

The river now curves steadily round further to the left. You soon find that the wind is "dead aft." Now is the time for care. As you continue swinging round to the left, you are gradually bringing the wind from your starboard quarter on to your port quarter; you are, in fact, on the way to change from sailing on the starboard gybe to sailing on the port gybe. As the boom holds the sail out, it is quite possible to continue sailing for some time with the wind a little on the port side of dead aft, but with the ship still on the starboard gybe. The ship is then said to be " by the lee," a ticklish situation. Suppose the wind shift a little bit further round to your port hand, or you cause its position to be shifted by continuing the curve or by not steering a dead true course, the wind may get under the corner of your sail and then "she gybes," the boom comes over uncontrolled, the main-sheet on its way picks off your new yachting cap and throws it in the river, and you may think yourself lucky if no further damage is done. Such a gybe may easily result in a broken boom or even in carrying away your mast. Better anticipate the ship's action, keeping it under control. Thus :—

Haul the main - sheet down flat. If the boom does not then come over, starboard your helm just a little bit, to get the wind the other side of the sail, and it will. Ease off the main-sheet, smoothly but as rapidly as you can—the jib can be left to take care of itself, as it probably has nothing to do just

now—and *look out to meet her with the helm.*
For when you were on the starboard gybe,
you carried starboard helm, because the ship
wanted to fly to starboard. The instant your
boom passed the midship line and the wind
was the other side of the sail, you were on
the port gybe and the ship wanted to fly
to port. This tendency must be checked *at
its birth.* You must be ready for it and meet
her *promptly* with port helm; otherwise she
will fly into the port-hand bank of the river.
Whence you will conclude that this evolution of gybing ship had better be carried
out, especially by the inexperienced, in mid-
stream. Take as much sea-room as you can
get in case of accidents, judge your wind
carefully and *gybe with deliberation.*

Having got her on her new gybe all safely,
you can trim your jib.

This is the beastliest of all manœuvres in
sailing. In narrow waters it is a deplorably
frequent necessity, and must be mastered.
The yachts sailed on the Broads have no gear
to get in the way, as is the case at sea. They
are rigged so that they may be gybed with
the least difficulty and danger, and the above
description applies only to them and their kind.

One last note on sailing with the wind aft. Don't forget that the boom is a long thing and, when the sheet is "all out," it takes up a lot of room. Keep an eye to see it does not go foul of anything—a passing yacht or a yacht at anchor, for instance. I have seen a man pass his main-sheet over a checking-post — the things they use to stop the big wherries—and the results to his mainsail were most lamentable. If you see an obstacle under your lee and cannot avoid it by easing your helm and going clear of it, *haul your main-sheet down flat* till you are past.

C.—Beating

The river now bends sharply round to the right. You execute another gybe from port to starboard gybe—"much better that time!" —you get down the main-sheet as the river continues to bend and the ship comes "by the wind." The wind is now well "forward of the beam," and the ship can just "lie" the next reach with all sheets as flat as possible. As the reach beyond turns still further to the right and we shall have to beat up it, and

as we want to sail as far as possible into
that reach without making a board, we let
her go now well into the windward bank,
with our weather eye (and *ear*) on the lookout for squalls and a firm hand on the helm.
As we come to the corner we ease the helm
slightly; but no, she won't "go any nearer."
A slight "lift" shows itself in the throat, and
the luff of the jib protests by shaking. We
can't fill the sails now by hauling any more
on the sheets. They are as far "home" as
we can profitably use them. So we up-helm
a bit and "lay her off," just enough to keep
that throat from lifting and the jib from
shaking. Herein lies the difficulty. As we
are going to windward we want to go as
near the wind as we can. But, if we sail
"too near the wind," we shall not make any
progress at all. The best guides are these:—
Watch the throat, which will give you warning
when you are getting too close. (Up-helm.)
Watch the burgee or weft at your masthead,
which will tell you if you are getting too
much "off the wind." (Ease the helm.)
Keep the ship moving through the water at
a good pace. The commonest fault in beating
to windward is "pinching her." Any boat

will "point" much nearer the wind than she will sail profitably. The point at which she will sail most advantageously varies with different boats, and can only be learned by experience. Keep her full and yet not too full, have the sheets pulled down flat, *but not too flat—you must give enough sheet to let the sails draw.* A mainsail with the boom nearly amidships does not drive the ship ahead. It only heels her over. If the ship is dragging slowly through the water, she is not making good work to windward, however "high" she may be pointing. She is "making heavy weather of it." Be generous to her; it will pay.

To go about; call "lee-oh" to your "crew," to let him know what you are about. ("All hands to their stations and the cook to the foresheet!") All he will have to do, in an up-to-date craft, is to ease the jib-sheet as she comes to the wind, let it go, and trim the other sheet when she is round. In older craft it was sometimes necessary to "pay her off" in order to get her round. With a single sheet he has nothing to do. Ease your helm and let her shoot directly into the wind. Don't let her lose her way and have to make a fresh start. But the instant she shows signs of losing liveliness, put the helm down—*gently*, pray—and get her going on her new course as fast as possible. You can "shoot" much further with a favourable than with an unfavourable tide. A foot gained directly to windward is worth yards of sailing obliquely. But don't overdo it.

The exactness with which you hit off the new course will be a test of your ability. Your mistakes are plainly written in the ship's wake behind you. If the wake goes out in a large curl on your weather quarter, it is telling you where you ought to have been and would have been had you not been so "heavy with the helm." To sail well to windward requires long practice and a "gift." A few hints like the above may be helpful. But no amount of writing will make the reader a sailor. So we will stow the jaw-tackle. Go thou. Do it. And discourse upon it after.

D.—Swing-bridges

Nothing tries the seamanship of the Broad sailor more than getting through the swing-

bridges which the railways have carried over
so many of the southern rivers. As you
approach the bridge, look out for the red flag
on it. When this flag is flying it means that
a train is expected and the bridge is " on."
You must delay matters. If the wind is aft,
pull down your main-sheet flat to take the
way off her. If that is not enough and you
get near the bridge, turn her round in the
river and make a few tacks to windward,
swing her round and come down to the
bridge again. Repeat the manœuvre as often
as may be necessary. Or beat back a little
way from the bridge, go to the windward
bank and hang on with the rond anchor.
If the wind is ahead, reverse the proceeding.

When the flag is hauled down, the bridge
is " off," and you can—all things being well
—get through.

If the wind is aft you can sail through,
taking care that your boom and your *gaff*
go clear of the lee side of the bridge.

If the wind is " free," that is, if you can
sail without any fear of being compelled to
go about, you can sail through, with a good
eye to getting your gaff clear. The gaff
sticks out a terrible long way aloft there and

it is quite easy to hook the peak of your mainsail on some projection and rend it.

If the wind is ahead, so that you have to beat, but is in such a direction that one of your "boards" is well up (or down) the river and the other across it, so that you are making "a long and a short leg," you must arrange to take the bridge on the long leg. As you go through you must ease the helm and let her shoot through, helping her with the quant if necessary (stand by the quant all ready in case); up-helm and sail her the moment she is clear. You will see a wherry shoot a bridge so with ease. But remember that your little yacht is not carrying some forty tons of cargo, and has not consequently the momentum to make her shoot like that.

A strong favourable tide will enable you to shoot the bridge nicely. A strong un-favourable tide may make it an impossibility even with the help of the quant. If wind and tide are both dead against you, you had better give it up and tie up in the bank until the tide eases or the wind changes, whichever shall first occur, as the lawyers say. If you *must* go through, lower away everything, the mast if necessary, and quant.

Lastly, if you have any doubt about your ability to sail or shoot through, *don't chance it*. Better be sure than sorry. Down sail and shove her through. No sailor will laugh at you for going on the safe side of things. The lubber who laughs will probably rend his mainsail on the next bridge he tackles. So don't mind him.

Beating to windward is the most difficult but the safest point of sailing; running is the easiest and most dangerous, but getting through the swing - bridges is the Devil. There is one thing worse—getting through Yarmouth.

Yarmouth has swing and fixed bridges and a tide like the rapids of Niagara. But it is quite easy to go through at slack water, very preferably low water slack. There can be no point in arriving at Yarmouth at high water. *Ascertain the time of low water slack* at Yarmouth and arrange to arrive there just *before*. Take your time and go through comfortably on the slack with the aid of the quant. I shall not tell you what to do at other times, because, if you don't know, you should not attempt it. If you do, then you don't need advice, and you probably will not.

Note on Balance-lugs. — The balance-lug
is a favourite sail in small craft, and is un-
questionably the handiest sail for a dinghy.
It becomes rather troublesome if it is large.
In setting it, get it up as taut as possible;
for there is not a direct pull to make the luff
taut, as in a cutter's mainsail, so that considerable power has to be employed to ensure
the luff being as taut as it is desirable that a
luff should be. Some balance-lugs have a plain
tack with a purchase on the halyard. You
will then make fast the tack so that the boom
goes a convenient height up the mast when
sail is set, and get the sail up "like a drum"
with the purchase on the halyard. Others
have a plain halyard and a purchase on the
tack. You will then hoist on the halyard
to a convenient height and set up the sail
by "bowsing down" on the tack till you
have the desired flatness.

The idea of a balance-lug is that the part
of the sail which is before the mast will do
the duty of a jib and balance the part which
is abaft the mast. All that has been said
about sailing a cutter or sloop applies equally
to a balance-lug. If you want to pay off
the head of a balance-lug boat, however, you

can use the sail as if it were a jib; hold the boom over to windward and make a backsail of the entire sail.

Note on Steering.—I have known a man unable to judge, when sitting to windward on a beamy boat, where his boat was heading. She would keep on edging up to windward. On my remonstrating with him, he declared that the boat was not heading where I said she was, but well to leeward of that position. I asked him how he judged. He said he took the line from his eye over the stem-head! And I had to explain that such a line, especially in a boat of wide beam, was very far from being parallel with the boat's midship line, and that he must find by his judgment a line *parallel to the boat's keel* in order to know where she was heading, which he seemed to have much difficulty in doing. Perhaps this note may be useful to others who have not become familiar with the helm. A pencil diagram will make the explanation very plain.

CHAPTER IV

ON STRONG WINDS AND REEFING

THERE are two kinds of people sailing: those who like to sail with comfort and without worry; and those who, while not racing, yet want to get along "as fast as they jolly well can." To both of these, with the beneficent object of aiding each to obtain his desire, I would say, "Don't carry too much sail."

The old hand, who knows his own craft, will come on deck in the morning, look at the weather, give a sniff and instantly say what sail is to be set. And indeed the sail to be set is a serious matter, only to be decided by mature judgment. What can one advise the tyro to do? One thing for certain. If he has any doubt whether to take down a reef or perhaps take down another, or one more than he first thought, to take it down. He will be on the safe side in the first place, and in the second place, it is much less trouble to pull up and shake out a reef than to pull up and take one down. Moreover, the disinclination to pull up and shake out a reef is not likely to lead to serious trouble, while the stronger disinclination to pull up and take one down may.

And let the tyro, who wants to go as fast as he jolly well can, remember that more sail does not necessarily mean more speed. His boat will slip along faster and with more comfort under a proper allowance of canvas, than if she is burying herself under a press of sail, "half seas over."

On the Broads it is not a bad guide to the tyro to watch the wherries, especially the business wherries. These carry one huge sail, increased by an extra breadth laced on at the bottom and called the "bonnet." When a wherryman takes off his "bonnet" it is time for you to take a reef. If he takes in one reef, you take two; and so on.

More sails are rent or otherwise ruined by improper reefing than in any other way. And the commonest method of destruction is this:—Lower your sail sufficiently, or hoist it, as the case may be, to let you get at the reef points, or at the eyelets through which you will lace it to the boom. (Practically all sails on smooth waters are laced to the boom; and the reef points or reef lacings are tied round the boom.) Tie the points or lace up the reef. Hoist and set your sail. When the sail fills, the strain comes on the points or the lacing, and, as the sail is not so made as to bear the strain imposed in this way, it starts rending at the point or eyelet where the strain is greatest. The rent spreads rapidly across the sail, and your sailing is over for some time to come. You have then discovered how *not* to do it. But it is surprising how many people make the discovery this way!

The strain on a sail is greatest at the corners and edges. That is why there is a rope sewn on there. When you take down a reef you must make use of that rope. In a line with the reef points or eyelets you will find, at either end of the reef, an eye fastened into the rope. One is called the "luff cringle," and the other, the after one, the "leech cringle." *These are the essential parts of the reef.* The reef points or lacing are only there to make the sail tidy—not to take the strain.

Set up the topping-lift; but not so high that you cannot easily reach the boom. Hoist (or lower, as the case may be) your sail to a convenient height for getting at the reef. Cast off as many mast-hoops as necessary. Unshackle the tack of the mainsail and shackle on the luff cringle. Or, as is often more convenient, take a piece of lacing three or four feet long and attach it to the luff cringle by two half-hitches or a bowline knot. Pass it through the tack shackle, or round the gooseneck, through the cringle again, and so on four or five times, at such a length that the luff cringle will be not higher than the upper side of the boom. Finish with a couple of half-hitches round all parts of the lacing. *Remember that this has to bear the strain of your getting the luff up taut.*

Now attach another bit of lacing, longer than the first, to the leech cringle. This is the " earing." Pass it through the hole in the boom. (The first reef earing goes through the hole farthest aft, and so on.) Through the cringle again. Do this twice, so that two parts show on either side the boom. Haul out on this till the new " foot" of the sail lies flat along the boom, but not so as to pull the sail out of shape. See that both parts of the earing are bearing an equal strain. Fold the slack part of the leech, that which is in the reef, forward along the boom, to be out of the way. Lash the cringle firmly on top of the boom with four or five turns of the earing round the boom and through the cringle. Finish off by bringing the end of the earing from the cringle to the part of the earing that passes through the hole in the boom and take two half-hitches round all parts. Twist the loose end of earing, that may remain, between the two strands of this part, for tidiness' sake. You have now "passed the earing," and your reef is secure.

Lastly, roll up the reef itself into a neat sausage on top of the boom and tie the points, or lace. In lacing, pass the lacing through all the eyelets, working from forward aft. Take care you *don't catch into it any part of the main-sheet*, which is sometimes led forward along the under side of the boom to be handy for the man in the well. Make fast the after end to the leech cringle or anything handy. Then pull the lacing taut, working from aft forward, keeping the reef neatly rolled, and make fast to the luff cringle or the gooseneck. Coil or otherwise make tidy the loose end.

Set sail.

To recapitulate. — The essential work of every reef in every kind of fore-and-aft sail is *making fast the cringles.* It is the omission of this, really the one thing necessary, that causes so much disaster. It is pitiful to see, as I have seen many, good sails ruined for want of this little bit of knowledge. Make fast the luff cringle first, whether your sail be mainsail, balance-lug or jib, then the leech cringle, drawing out the foot nicely, but not straining it. Lastly, make up the reef tidily with the points or the lacing. These hints should enable you to reef any sail you may meet with on inland waters with safety to the sail.

If you reef your mainsail much, say two reefs or more, you should either reef your jib too, or set a smaller jib; otherwise you will perhaps destroy that balance between the sails referred to on p. 16.

Shaking out a Reef

Cast off the lacing or untie the points; and be sure they are *all* untied, or the sail will be rent when you hoist. *Set up the topping-lift,* or the boom will fall when you cast off the earing. Cast off the tack or the luff cringle. Shackle on the main tack, if it has been cast off, or make it fast, if a shackle is not used. Cast off the earing. Set the sail. Lash on the mast-hoops. Let go topping-lift. Trim the sheet.

If the wind, though strong, be steady, you will reef accordingly. If it be squally, *reef for the squalls*, not for the lulls, nor for a mean between the two. You are not racing, and you don't want to risk breaking anything. You may, nevertheless, be caught in a squall with rather more sail than you want. Let us consider a squall under three heads.

1. *With a head wind.*—Ease your helm and let her go closer to the wind. This will let the squall strike the sails at an acuter angle, and will consequently not have so much effect on the ship as if the squall struck her broadside on. Letting the ship go thus towards the wind is called "luffing." A squall, so treated, actually helps you to go to windward. *But*, be ready to ease both sheets, jib and mainsail, if the squall should prove too heavy for you. For you cannot allow her to remain head to wind to avoid the squall, because she might become unmanageable and

go ashore. You must keep her going.
Therefore NEVER MAKE YOUR SHEETS FAST IN
SUCH A WAY THAT YOU CANNOT CAST THEM
OFF INSTANTLY. I have seen a yacht, from
lack of this precaution, lie down in the river,
fill and sink. The party on board walked
ashore by the mast, quite safe, but uncomfortable and undignified. Some people get
drowned that way. In open boats, never
make your main-sheet fast *in any way*. Hold
it in your hand.

2. *Wind abeam.*—In a river there is not
room to luff. So ease your sheets, and let
the wind out of your sails. Keep her straight
with the helm.

3. *Wind aft.*—Keep her straight and pray
that it may not be necessary to gybe during
the squall. If the squall is very heavy, or
threatens to be very heavy, top the boom by
the topping-lift and lower the peak. This
"scandalises" the mainsail.

If the squalls continue, let her come "by
the wind" (down - helm), get her to the
windward bank and anchor (*see* chap. vi.).
Lower away everything, if necessary. Take
down a reef or reefs, as may be necessary,
and make a fresh start.

Sudden squalls are very common in all inland sailing, especially if there be hills in the neighbourhood. In Norfolk they are known as "Rogers." At sea, you can see a squall coming over the water. On a river you can't usually see much beyond the bank. But you can generally *hear* a Roger coming over the marsh, and be ready for him when he arrives. Keep your weather *ear* open!

One last piece of advice. Never put your feet on the main-sheet or any other sheet. The main-sheet should always be free for running, as aforesaid. If it is not so, there is danger. Moreover, many and many a good man has been drowned by getting foul of the main-sheet when the accident happened. So don't *start* foul of anything, and the main-sheet in particular. And *compel* your crew and passengers to observe the rule too. If they laugh, they don't know anything about it. Compel them, even if it have to be with a rope's end or a belaying pin!

CHAPTER V

ON THE RULE OF THE ROAD

THE precepts given in a previous chapter, on Sailing, would be delightfully simple and straightforward in practice, if nothing got in the way to complicate matters. But, as we don't have the sea, or even the Broads, to ourselves, it is just as well to know how to avoid collision with the other people. And here the Board of Trade comes to our assistance.

The Rule of the Road goes on the principle that the vessel which has things all her own way shall give way to the vessel that is comparatively in difficulties, except in two cases where an arbitrary rule is unavoidable.

Article 17 [1] of the Regulations says :—

"When two sailing vessels are approaching one another, so as to involve risk of collision, *one* of them shall keep out of the way of the other, as follows : viz. :—

"*Article* 17*a*.—A vessel which is running free shall keep out of the way of a vessel going close-hauled."

---

[1] A black line indicates that the rule is of frequent application in narrow waters.

You are close-hauled when you are sailing as near the wind as you can sail. But if you find that you could *sail*, not *point*, nearer the wind than you are doing, you must consider yourself as "free," although the wind may be a little forward of the beam. The situation described in 17*a*, though common enough at sea, does not often occur in narrow waters, except in the case of a vessel before the wind meeting one which is beating to windward— a case to be dealt with under 17*e*.

Article 17*b*.—" A vessel which is close-hauled on the port tack shall keep out of the way of a vessel which is close-hauled on the starboard tack."

This is an arbitrary distinction, but unavoidable. And so likewise with

Article 17*c*.—" When both are running free, with the wind on different sides, the vessel which has the wind on the port side shall keep out of the way of the other."

This is a situation frequently occurring in narrow waters, where boats may be meeting "end on," having the wind abeam or nearly so.

Article 17*d*.—" When both are running free, with the wind on the same side, the vessel which is to windward shall keep out of the way of the vessel that is to leeward."

This rule is intended to deal with vessels

whose courses cross one another, and not to
vessels sailing on identical or parallel courses.
It will therefore not apply in narrow waters
at all, except possibly at a confluence of
rivers.

Article 17e.—" A vessel which has the wind aft shall keep out
of the way of the other vessel."

A very common situation in narrow waters.
When you are approaching another vessel,
make up your mind as soon as possible with
which of you lies the responsibility of getting
clear of the other.   Has "the other" any
responsibility at all, or may she just go where
and how she pleases ?   The answer is

Article 21.—" Where by any of these Rules one of two vessels is
to keep out of the way, *the other shall keep her course and speed.*
NOTE.—When in consequence of thick weather or other causes *
such vessel finds herself so close that collision cannot be avoided
by the action of the giving-way vessel alone, she also shall take
such action as will best aid to avert collision."

* [*Among which we may class the ignorance of those who will not learn.*]

Article 29 adds to this that every vessel
must keep a proper lookout and take proper
precautions *in all circumstances*.   So that
you cannot consider yourself absolved from
responsibility even if you are sailing close-
hauled on the starboard tack.   You may be
called upon to get out of the way of a boat

which has just gone round to clear the bank and is now on port tack while you are still on starboard. For *Article* **27** says :—

" In obeying and construing these Rules, due regard shall be had to all dangers of navigation and collision, and to any special circumstances which may render a departure from the above Rules necessary in order to avoid immediate danger."

All this looks very alarming and confusing on paper. But with reasonable care you will not often in practice find any departure from the ordinary Rules necessary, except in the case suggested above, to which we will return later.

Article 22.—" Every vessel which is directed by these Rules to keep out of the way of another vessel shall, if the circumstances of the case admit, avoid crossing ahead of the other."

In other words, don't go across the other fellow's bows if you can help it. Go under his stern.

Article 24.—" Notwithstanding anything contained in these Rules, every vessel, overtaking any other, shall keep out of the way of the overtaken vessel."

A Rule of constant application.

Article 20.—" When a steam vessel and a sailing vessel are proceeding in such directions as to involve risk of collision, the steam vessel shall keep out of the way of the sailing vessel."

A steamer may be, in fact, regarded as having the wind aft. But you must bear in mind that steamers sometimes draw a lot of water, and by *Articles* 27 and 29 they are absolved from the necessity of putting themselves ashore simply in order to avoid your imperial sail. Moral: don't get in the way of a steamer unless you must.

The Rules say nothing about rowing boats, which are regarded, I presume, as beyond the pale of reason and discipline. There is nothing in the Rules, however, to justify running into them. So it is as well to avoid doing it.

Those, I think, are all the rules which are applicable to sailing the Broads. *Article* 30 makes a special reservation for rules made in harbours and rivers by local authority. Keep a weather eye lifting for these rare birds on entering any strange harbour. You will probably receive timely notice.

The careful reader will have observed that in narrow waters it almost always happens that vessels are necessarily sailing *on the same courses*, though it may be in opposite directions, at the time they meet. At very sharp corners, such as occur at the confluence of two streams, ships may meet at an angle and the Rule of the Road may have to be hastily applied, because each vessel is probably about to alter her course suddenly at the corner. There remains, of course, the very familiar problem of a vessel with the wind aft having to clear another, or perhaps others, going to windward.

And now, as the preacher says, for the practical application.

The situations may, practically, be reduced to four.

1. *Meeting end on.*—*Article* 17c provides for ninety-nine out of one hundred cases. Port tack gets out of the way. Starboard tack stands on. *Article* 17a provides for the odd case. If you have the wind well aft of the beam and the other man is getting "pinched" for wind, keep out of his way and give him a chance. Pass to leeward of him. This is obedient to *Article* 22, and also courteous. If you are really close-hauled, you may expect the other man to do as much for you.

2. *Overtaking.*—Wind free or aft. There are a lot of rules for this in racing. But you are not racing. You are only, as the celebrated bus-driver said, "going as fast as you jolly well can." So you won't shove your way between the overtaken vessel and the

windward bank. You will go past him which-ever way gives most room. And he must remember that the Rules expect him not to alter his course (*Article* 21), not even for the sake of courtesy. Politeness is very nice and costs nothing ashore. It may be very dangerous on the water and cost a good deal. Stick to the Rules.

3. *Crossing in beating to windward.* — This will occur when you overtake another vessel, both of you going to windward. You are not now, however, an "overtaking vessel," "within the meaning of the act." You are a meeting or crossing vessel, and subject to *Article* 17*b* and *Articles* 22 and 27.

Getting past another vessel when you are both beating to windward in a narrow channel requires so much seamanship and is subject to such complications in practice that it is impossible to give any fixed instruction. Remember that port tack has to give way to starboard tack, but is not bound to put himself ashore, to "pile himself up," in order to do so. Starboard tack must bear this in mind.

The following hints may be of use. They

illustrate the principle of getting by. But they must be used with such modifications as are necessitated by the various circumstances of each case.

When you overtake a vessel turning to windward, try to arrange that you "go about" on opposite sides of the river. Try also to arrange so that the first time you meet him *you* shall be on port tack. Up-helm and go close *under his stern*, letting your boat come by the wind the instant you are past by easing your helm. [*N.B.*— Don't cut it too fine, and remember his gaff sticks out a long way, and that as he passes to windward of you, and takes your wind, you will for the moment come upright. Close *under his stern*, not close alongside of him.] * The next time you go about you will be on starboard tack and he on port. You should also, being the faster ship, be so far advanced that he can easily go under your stern. And, if you continue to make favourable progress, you may be able to sail clear of him next board, when you are on port tack. But don't go across his bows unless you are *sure* you can go clear. Go about. Let us now return to *. Perhaps you have not advanced so far as to enable him to go under your stern. He will then have to go about to avoid you, making a "short board." Watch him carefully now, *though* you are on starboard tack, for he will have to go about to avoid going into the bank, and will, in so doing, come across your bows on port tack. Your best plan is to go about just *before* he does, and try to sail past and round him on the next reach and turn to windward. His short board will have brought you into just that position that you tried at first to avoid, viz.: both boats going about at the same time and on the same side of the river.

The whole manœuvre is frequently further complicated by the fact that one of the boats usually "points" higher than the other, or is longer "in stays," *i.e.*, in coming round. If the overtaken vessel is in the hands of a sailor and you are not racing, as aforesaid, he will make it easy for you to get by. But if her Palinurus "knows nothing about it," I can only say, "use your utmost diligence and skill, and trust in Providence."

4. *Wind aft, meeting a vessel or vessels beating.*—This is the most familiar of all these

problems. It is your duty to keep clear; the other man's to keep on working as if you were not there, but with a careful eye on you all the while (*Articles* 17*e* and 29). Your best plan is as follows :—

Go to the middle of the river. As you approach the other vessel, point your ship directly at her, so as to have the best chance of passing whichever side you wish. Then try to arrange that you shall pass under his stern between him and the bank he has just left, when he last went about. If you can't do this, *give him a wide berth* the other side.

Don't go across his bows just as he has gone about. If you do, then either he must hang his ship in the wind till you have gone by, which is an inconvenience to which you had neither the right nor need to put him, or—there is a smash and you are primarily responsible.

Finally, whatever you do, do deliberately and in plenty of time, *so that the other man can see your intention.* Don't take unnecessary risks — it is not war time. Don't cut things fine — you are not racing. Also, the Rules come first, politeness second.

CHAPTER VI

MOORING, STOWING, AWNINGS, DOWN-MAST

I REMEMBER lying at anchor at Acle, moored to the windward bank. Personally I have a preference for the windward bank. It is easy to get under way from it, and the water does not make so much noise lapping against the ship's side all night as it does on the other bank.

The wind was blowing obliquely, down and across the river. Presently there appeared a yacht, bowling along bravely, main-sheet nearly all out and a fine smother of spray under her lee-bow—a gallant sight. There were many yachts lying moored to the lee bank, but amongst them was one nice empty berth. The new arrival, seeing this enticing spot under his lee, instantly made up his mind to occupy it. So he put his helm hard up and ran bang into the bank and a few feet up it.

54

He did not carry away his mast! A good stick that!

Instantly his ship began to swing round, as the tide was running down the river too. This brought the wind on his other quarter. Not quite blind to the situation, he noticed that his boom was about to come over. He avoided it with remarkable agility, but miscalculated the size of his little deck, and discovered about ten feet of water where he proposed to moor.

That is how not to do it.

Always try to arrive at your mooring just as the yacht loses her way. If you *must* moor on the lee-shore—you may have to for convenience of going ashore or some other good reason—get all the way off your ship before you get close to the bank, and let her drop gently into her berth broadside on.

I. Suppose you have the wind on the beam or forward of it: to get way off the ship, top your boom a little, drop your peak, ease off all sheets; the sails being now "spilt," she will soon lose her way. Steer her gently alongside into her berth, step ashore and make fast. If the tide is with you, anchor with the after rond anchor first, and *vice versa.* Otherwise she may swing round and give trouble.

II. If the wind is aft, swing her round as described in chap. ii. p. 19, make a board towards your berth, spill your sails and drop into your berth as above.

Always try to moor head to wind. It is easier to get under way again. It is much more comfortable in the well and cabin, especially if there is any rain.

But, other things being equal, make for the windward bank. Give her plenty of room to shoot; spill your sails and let her shoot into the wind, judging your speed and distance so that she will have lost her way just as her stem touches the bank. If you have much too much way on, yaw her about a bit to take it off. But she probably won't hit the bank very hard with the wind ahead. It requires considerable practice to judge the distance a boat will shoot with nicety. The amateur usually underestimates what his craft will do.

Have the rond anchor ready on the fore-deck *with the end of the rope made fast.* The instant she touches, step ashore, stick in your anchor and come aboard again. She will now lie quiet, head to wind, in a position which makes lowering and stowing your sail a much easier performance than it would be in the other bank. Everything you lower goes into its place, instead of blowing overboard.

Down-jib.—Lower your jib at once, if you did not do so when you put your helm down to let her shoot; which would have been *the* thing to do. If your jib is on a bowsprit, let go the outhaul first and pull the jib—if it doesn't fly in of its own accord—in along the bowsprit. Get your arms round it and "muzzle" it, to keep it quiet. Let go halyards and haul down. Unshackle halyard and jib-sheets, unhook the tack. Make fast the ends of the halyard, and lay the jib so that it won't blow overboard. If your "jib" is really a staysail, with no bowsprit, lower it, muzzling as it comes down, and stow temporarily as above.

Down-mainsail.—Top your boom slightly, if you have not already done so. Belay the lift conscientiously. Haul taut the main-sheet and belay. Lower your peak slightly, then peak and throat together. If the peak won't come down, haul on the downhaul or the ensign halyard or, in the absence of these, *with care* on the leech of the sail. If the throat sticks, haul down by the luff rope. (In very large craft, a Brixham trawler, for instance, a man goes aloft, stands on the jaws of the gaff, and overhauls the throat halyard as the sail comes down.)

Stow mainsail.—I. The jaws being down, lower the peak level with the boom. Take the leech of the sail and lay it forward along the top of the boom as far as it will go. Get all the sail on that side of the boom which is opposite to the peak.

Lash the peak to the boom firmly, rolling up that part of the sail which is aftside the tyer neatly on to the top of the boom. If you do this *now*, you won't have to cast off the peak tyer to put it right afterwards. Pass a lacing round the bunt of the sail to keep it quiet.

II. Ship the crutches. Lower the boom gently into them, remembering to let go the peak halyard as well as the topping-lift.

Haul taut the main-sheet again and belay. Belay the topping-lift, but don't let it take the weight of the boom off the crutches.

III. To roll up the mainsail cast off the lacing. The leech should lie along the top of the boom as aforesaid. Take hold of the

under part of the sail and throw the bunt
into it, as into a hammock. Shake it in well.
Take hold again, "another skin," and shake
in again. Proceed thus until the whole mainsail is tightly rolled in a long neat sausage on
top of the boom. Tie with the tyers or lace
it up so that it stays there.

Unshackle the halyards. The neatest way
to make fast is to hook the shackle of each,
without turns aloft, to its own cleat and belay
the fall. *Don't haul taut;* because if there is
rain in the night the halyards will "take up"
and be subjected to a strain which will "take
the life out of the rope."

Make a lacing fast to one leg of the
crutches. Pass it under the boom, over
(forward of the topping-lift), and make fast
to the other leg. The crutches cannot then
get adrift.

IV. Always, when stowing is complete,
slightly overhaul the topping-lift. You don't
want it to hang in a bight like a clothes-line;
but if you set it up a trifle too taut, the rain
or even the night dew may set it fully up
The weight of the boom and sail being thus
removed, the crutches slip silently overboard
during the night and make their escape on

the tide.   Securing them as above advised will, however, prevent any regrettable profanity on this account.

V. Put on the sail cover, beginning at the mast.   Lace up the part in front of the mast, and tie the upper lacing, which should be a long one, tightly round the mast over the cover, so that wet cannot run down the mast inside the cover.   Lace up the under side, pulling the cover out taut to make it sit neatly.   Lace it so that the main-sheet is still free, if it is carried along under the boom.

Should your mainsail be dripping wet, it is no use putting on the sail cover to keep it dry. But the mainsail will drip, and if the rain continues, go on dripping into your well, to your discomfort.   Therefore, lace the sail cover on *upside down*.   It will so make a gutter which will shoot all the water on to your cabin-top and foredeck, where it will do no harm.   You must manage the part in the way of the main-sheet as best you can.   Any device is good enough to minimise the discomforts caused by a dripping mainsail.

Cast off the main-sheet.   With a double part, take a couple of half-hitches round the standing part, to keep it taut and keep the boom down in the crutches. Coil the fall on one head of the crutches, where it will look pretty and be out of the way.

VI. If the jib has no boom, fold the clew to and just beyond the luff and then roll neatly. Leave the luff clear and the clew just sticking out. "Stop" it with a few pieces of yarn and stow it (in the sail-locker or forepeak).

If it has a boom, "flake" the luff up and down the boom, roll up the bunt, stop it and stow (on the cabin-top under the main-boom is a handy place for a jib of this kind).

If you have a single jib-sheet, unreeve it and coil neatly.

VII. To prevent that terrible tapping noise at night, which makes sleep impossible, with the fall of the jib halyard take three or four turns round all halyards and the mast, hauling taut. Belay. That will keep them quiet. But don't do this before you rig your awning.

VIII. Take your after rond anchor and go ashore. Pull her stern in, put in your anchor. If the wind has a tendency up or down stream, or if you think it likely to veer so, moor her so that she shall lie with her head to windward. Come aboard and find out with the quant, or an oar, what sort of bottom you have got. If you go alongside a bank at high tide and the bottom is not far off and shelves gradually, you may find yourself trying to roll over into the river during the night. This is not a very frequent condition, but one that is always worth watching.

If there is any danger, fix the point of the quant firmly into the shore, shove her well out, and " seize " the quant to the shrouds with twine. This will keep her out.

Make your mooring ropes fast now at a proper length, allowing for rise and fall of the tide, if any, and see that both go fair to the rond anchors, that the forward one, for instance, is not round the forestay and chafing it.

You may, however, find yourself wishing to anchor in some delightful Broad, where the shore is bad landing or inaccessible or away from the view. Of course you will avoid anchoring in the " fairway." If, as is probable in Norfolk, your ship does not boast an anchor, at any rate she probably owns a weight, which will hold well in the mud. I have ridden out a gale of wind to a 28-lb. weight on a warp in nice deep mud.

First select the spot where you wish to ride, and remember that a ship does not ride directly over her anchor, but — leaving tide out of the question—a distance to leeward of it. Therefore, second, select the place where you will drop your "anchor." When you anchor, you will allow about four times the depth of the water as the amount of warp to pay out. If you are using an anchor and chain cable, three times will be sufficient.

Remember that boats swing at the end of a cable. Don't choose your anchorage so that there is a danger of swinging or sheering foul of another vessel. The other ship sheers too.

Get your warp and "anchor" ready on the foredeck. Bend on the warp with an "anchor-bend" (chap. vii. p. 80). You have now to get to leeward of where you will drop your anchor and shoot her up to it, so that she will have lost all her way just as she arrives at the spot. Before you shoot, down-jib, and set up the topping-lift. Some modern craft are very lively and will give a lot of trouble in coming to an anchor unless you quiet them down.

When all the way is off, preferably when she begins to go astern, drop your anchor, pay out the necessary amount of warp and make fast. Lower away as soon as convenient. If you are using an anchor and chain cable, be sure she is making a little sternway before you let go, and pay the cable out slowly. To let your cable go plump down on top of your anchor is to invite a " foul anchor " which will drag ; because the chain starts pulling at the flukes instead of at the ring on the end of the shank.

What to do with the dinghy often becomes a question, as both wind and tide may make her bump against the yacht and disturb your sleep, to say nothing of the yacht's varnish. Some people make her fast stem and stern under the bowsprit shrouds. This is all right when you have bowsprit shrouds. A good place for her is under the after mooring rope, between the yacht and the bank. Make her painter fast to the shrouds. She will be quite quiet there.

Bring your awning on deck. Make the forward, which should also be the windward, end fast first. Don't tie the upper lacing round the halyards, but round the mast under

the halyards.   Set up the spreaders, keeping
the horizontal bars *outwards*.   (The heads
of the vertical bars would chafe the canvas.)
Fold the awning back along the boom, re-
versing the process of chap. ii. p. 6.   Haul
the ridge taut and make fast with the lacing.
Tie the points or lace, hauling taut.   As you
make fast in the way of the spreaders, press
the spreaders inwards slightly, so as to set
up a strain against the awning.   The end
flaps may be folded under between the roof
and the spreaders till they are wanted.

If the awning is wet, do not touch it or
the wet will come through.   A good awning,
if untouched, will keep out any weather.
The man who touches it should be made to
sit under the spot he has touched.

As the sun goes down, the time of which
will be regulated by the senior yacht on the
station, haul down the burgee, take it off
the halyard, and stow it till eight bells of
the morning watch (8 A.M.), when you will
hoist again ; again taking time from the
senior yacht.   On the Broads this ceremony
is as much honoured in the breach as in
the observance.   It is not the fault of the
ceremony.

Notice how the stick of the burgee is made fast to the halyard—by slipping on those half-hitches which are described in the next chapter, p. 78.

Down-mast.—It is necessary on waters where there are fixed bridges to lower the mast. Also, in small craft, if anything goes wrong aloft, don't go there to put it right unless you must. If you can, lower the mast.

A mast made to lower is not " stepped " and wedged. It is " housed " in a " tabernacle." This is a sort of wooden box with the fore-side open. Through the upper part and the mast passes a big " fid " or bolt, on which the mast swings. When the mast is up it is secured by a bar, usually with a ring on one end and a hook on the other, across the front of the lower part of the tabernacle, and it is held in position by the shrouds and the forestay. When the mast is lowered, the foot swings up through the forehatch, the cover of which slides off.

I. *Prepare to down-mast.* Come to an anchor. Lower your sails. Pass the peak tyer and put a lacing on the bunt. Ascertain whether the bridge is high enough to allow you to pass with boom and mast in the crutches. It often will not. If that is the case, it is no use shipping the crutches. Everything will have to be lowered on to the cabin-top.

Always have your cabin-top, if of the " lifting " variety, down during these operations.

Lay your boom to one side, sufficiently to be clear of the mast. Cast off the parrel. (A parrel is any rope holding a spar against a mast. In a cutter it is the lacing which joins the jaws of the gaff across the front of the mast. Its chief office is to prevent the halyards from getting nipped in the jaws. It is provided with " parrel-balls.") When you cast it off, make a knot in the end or otherwise secure the balls. If they go into the river, you ought to feel it your duty to buy new ones. Cast off the halyards and make fast.

Lay the gaff on the same side as the boom, having unshipped the jaws from the mast.

Slide off the forehatch and see there is nothing in the way of the foot of the mast.

II. Unhook the bar across the tabernacle. If the mast is so firm against it that you cannot move it, a good swig on the forestay should bring it to reason.

Some masts are fitted with counterpoises, heavy weights at the foot, to give a nice balance; some with a foot-tackle.

Cast off the foot-tackle if there be one. Cast off the forestay-tackle. But stand by either the foot-tackle or the forestay-tackle to steady the mast as it is lowered. Let one hand stand by this and the other haul on the topping-lift or other part of the gear to start the mast, and then stand by to catch and steady her on the last part of her downward path.

Put a lacing round all parts of the gear to keep it clear of the tiller, and you are ready to shove through the bridge.

Up-mast.—I. Cast off the lacing round the gear. See that nothing can go foul. You will not always succeed, but do your best. Usually the shrouds go foul of the ends of the cabin-top or a halyard embraces the helm. Remove it patiently and try again. Don't swear. It's about as much use as a headache.

II. One hand mans the foot-tackle or the forestay-tackle, as the case may be. The other stands on the cabin-top to start the mast with a lift. As soon as the foot is well home, secure it with the bar. Set taut and belay the forestay-tackle. Coil the fall neatly. Belay or stow the foot-tackle. Close the forehatch. Ship the jaws of the gaff and make fast the parrel.

III. Top the boom and prepare to make sail.

Yachts usually anchor to down- and up-mast. Wherries, being simply rigged with this special object, down-mast, shoot the bridge, and up-mast again under way. The amateur is advised not to try this game with a yacht's gear, but to anchor. Again— *it is better to be sure than sorry.*

CHAPTER VII

ABOUT KNOTS

[*N.B.*—Don't practise with string. Get a bit
of lacing or very stout string, $\frac{1}{8}$ inch
diameter at least.]

A KNOWLEDGE of how to tie knots is
necessary to the sailor and handy for every
one. We will, therefore, devote a chapter
to the subject — not an exhaustive one, so
there is no need for alarm. We will confine
ourselves to a few knots which are absolutely
necessary for any one taking charge of anything larger than a toy boat.

You may divide the knots into classes,
thus :—

    (*a*) Simple knots and loops.
    (*b*) Knots for uniting ropes.
    (*c*) Knots for making fast the ends of ropes.
    (*d*) Splices.
    (*e*) Service.

(a) *Simple knots.*—These are usually employed to stop a rope from passing through a hole through which you don't want it to pass. The simplest form is the overhand knot—an old friend under, to the landsman, an unfamiliar name. It is just a "knot" (see Fig. 1). Don't use it. If it is subjected to any strain it "jams" and is hard to untie. If you want to stop your jib-sheet, for instance,

Fig. 1 Overhand Knot   Fig 2 Flemish Knot

from running all out through the "lead" in the coaming of the well, tie a Flemish, *alias* figure-of-eight, knot (Fig. 2). It won't jam so hard, and is consequently comparatively easy to untie.

Loops.—The most useful loop at the end of a rope is a "bowline knot." If you want a slip knot, tie a "running bowline."

Before we try to describe the tying of a "bowline," let us know the parts of a rope (see Fig. 3). The "standing part" is the part you can't monkey with, because it comes direct from the coil, or because it is made fast to something, or because you please to assume one of these conditions. A "bight" is a festoon (see Dictionary). An "end" is an end (see common-sense).

Bowline knot.—Take the standing part in your left hand, the end towards you. With

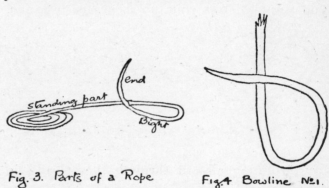

Fig. 3. Parts of a Rope   Fig.4 Bowline №1.

your right hand lay the end over the standing part, so forming a bight, which will be the loop when the knot is made. Let the end point over the standing part towards your left (Fig. 4).

Now for the secret. Lay the forefinger of your right hand on the point where the end crosses the standing part. Take hold of both parts with your right forefinger and thumb,

having your thumb *inside* the bight. Grip
firmly and turn your hand over, so that the
thumb comes on top. This twist will have
formed a little bight, or kink, at the crossing
point, through which the end will have passed
automatically with the twist of your hand.
You now have Fig. 5.

Now pass the end *under* the standing part,
and, bringing it up, pass it *down* through
the "little bight." That's it ! (Fig. 6.)

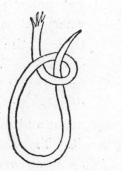 

Fig 5. Bowline. Nº 2   Fig 6 Bowline Nº 3,

I have seen other weird descriptions of how
to tie a bowline. But this is the seaman's
way. It is the easiest and quickest. The
great secret is in the *twist* above described.

A bowline knot will not slip, cannot jam,
and is easily untied. A "running bowline"

is this knot so tied that its bight is round the standing part. You thus have a slip knot, with the bowline as the running knot. It won't jam and can be readily cast off.

(*b*) *Uniting ropes.*—The handiest knot for uniting two ropes is the "common bend." Form an eye on one end; pass the other end

through the eye, round both parts of the eye, and under itself where it comes through the eye (Fig. 7). You may, if you like, double it; pass

Fig. 7 Common Bend

it round the parts of the eye again and under itself again before you harden it. This makes it less liable to jam. *If the ropes are of different sizes make the eye on the stouter.*

Reef knot.—Never tie two ropes together with a reef knot; it cannot be trusted. There is a popular superstition that it can. This is a fallacy. It is very liable to slip. If the ropes are of different sizes it is certain to. Its chief uses are for tying your bootlaces, joining the ends of lacings, and tying up reef

points. And it should not be used for other
purposes. To tie it, see Figs. 8 and 9. The

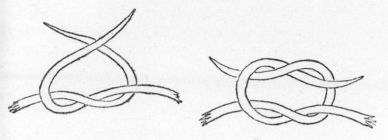

Fig 8 Reef Knot. Nº 1.   Fig. 9. Reef Knot. Nº 2

"granny" is the result of forgetting that ends
should not change their direction in good
knots—they should keep on going round the
same way. In a
"granny" the
ends are wrongly
crossed (Fig. 10).
The ends of a reef
knot lie in a line
with the standing
parts: the ends of
a granny at right
angles to them.

Fig. 10. 'Granny' begun.

(c) *Making fast: Belaying.* — Learn a
standard method of belaying and never depart

7

from it. You can then always belay or cast
off automatically in a second. The ability to
do so may avert an accident.

Belay thus :—Take a round turn, two cross
turns, and a round turn to finish. Let us
explain :—

1. A round turn is once completely round
the neck of the cleat. Suppose, for instance,

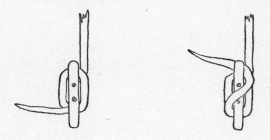

Fig. 11. A Round Turn.   Fig. 12. One cross Turn.

you are belaying a halyard. The standing
part comes down to the cleat. Take a round
turn, going, of course, " the way of the sun ";
the same direction as the hands of your watch;
the same way that you pass, or ought to pass,
the bottle. The end will now be to your left
(Fig. 11).

2. Take the end upwards across the cleat,
(Fig. 12), and then downwards across (Fig. 13),

and you have two cross turns. The first cross turn is always back towards the standing-part; if it does not come so, there is something wrong with your round turn.

3. Take a final round turn on top of all and the rope is belayed.

The clove hitch.—This is a knot of universal

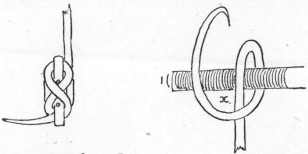

Fig 13. Second Cross Turn   Fig. 14. Clove Hitch. Nº 1.

application and turns up in as many forms as Proteus. Practise it for a start on a horizontal rail. First, with the standing part coming from behind you and the end pointing out in front of you, pass the end over the rail, down-round, and over again, crossing the first turn (Fig. 14). Bringing the end down-round, pass it through the opening *x* (Fig. 14), producing Fig. 15. This is a clove hitch. Notice that the end goes round the spar *always in the same direction*.

You may now take a "half-hitch" round
the standing part with the end and the knot
will bear anything. Fig. 16 shows the complete knot with parts loose, for clearness' sake.

Next try the knot again, having the standing part in front of you and the end coming
towards you; all the movements are exactly
reversed. Then try it on an upright post.

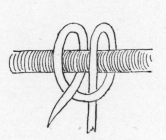
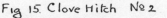
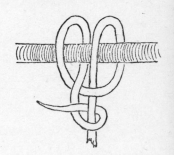

Fig 15. Clove Hitch No 2   Fig 16 Clove Hitch. No 3.

Now take any free spar, a cricket stump
or even a pencil. Tie the knot, minus the
final half-hitch. Slip it off and examine it.
You will see it consists of two half-hitches
(Fig. 17). Try to form these half-hitches on
an end and slip them one at a time on to
a spar, so that they will form a clove hitch.
To slip two such half-hitches over the head
of a stump is the quickest way of making a

rope fast, tying up a dinghy, for instance. The art is worth acquiring.

A rolling bend.—Very useful for making fast. Take two (or more) turns round the

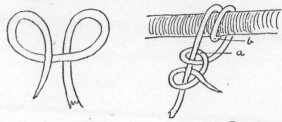

Fig. 17. Clove Hitch, dissected   Fig. 18. Rolling Bend

spar and then two half-hitches round the standing part, Fig. 18. Often used instead of a clove hitch.

Anchor bend. — This knot (Fig. 19) is a noble descendant of the last. It is made by passing the end under the second turn on the spar in making the first half-hitch, *a* under *b* (Fig. 18). Finish with the second half-hitch, and you have an "anchor" or "topsail

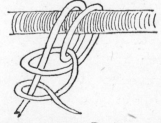

Fig 19 Anchor Bend

halyard" bend. It is a good knot to make fast to a ring, or to a spar. Hence the names.

Much practice is necessary to make these knots really familiar, so that they are tied more by an exercise of habit than of thought. But a familiar knowledge of these is the minimum for any one desiring to deserve the name of sailor. Those who desire, very properly, to know more, will find the information in any good work on rigging.

(*d*) *Splices.*—The aim of this book being brevity, we will confine ourselves to those things which are matters of everyday occurrence. Very seldom does the boat-sailor find himself called upon to join two pieces of rope with a splice. He usually gets along without so doing. But he oftens finds it desirable to splice an "eye" at the end of a rope, so the process shall be described.

An eye-splice.—Unlay—that is untwist the strands of—the rope, so that you have a convenient length of strand to work with. Four or five inches will do nicely for a 1-inch rope (note that rope is measured by circumference and not by diameter). Form your "eye" of the size you want. Take a marline-

spike—a shackle-spike or a "pricker" is large
enough for a 1-inch rope, but anything with
a point will do; I am at this moment using a
pencil point to make an eye-splice in a 1-inch
rope to draw the illustrations from—and lift
a strand at the
point where the
"eye" is to be
made. Lay the
end on the stand-
ing part in the
position advised
for starting a
bowline (Fig. 4).
Put the middle
end under the
lifted strand, a
under i (Fig.
20).

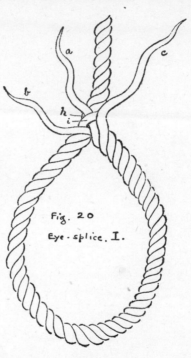

Fig. 20
Eye-splice. I.

Turn the eye
towards your
right and lift
the next strand,
putting the pricker under it where the last
end emerges (Fig. 20, h). Put the left hand
end, (20 b) under this.

Still turning your eye towards the right,

lay it on its back, so to speak. The splice should now appear as in Fig. 21. Raise the strand *d*, putting the pricker under it at *e*, from your right hand. Bring the end *c* over and put it under *d* in the same direction as you used the pricker, *from your right*. This is the crucial point of the eye - splice. The splice should now appear as in Fig. 22.

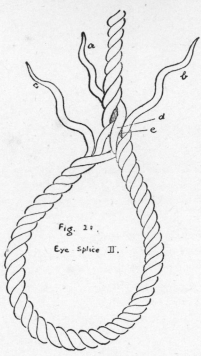

Fig. 21.

Eye Splice II.

All that now has to be done is to "lay the ends in" under the strands of the standing part. If you look down on the eye from the standing part you will see that the three ends project regularly between the three strands of the standing part. To "lay them in," raise the next strand but one and put the end under it, as nearly at right angles to the lay of the rope as it will go. Don't lay in any end twice till every end has been laid in once. In Fig. 22, *b* must go under *f*, *c* under *g*, and so on.

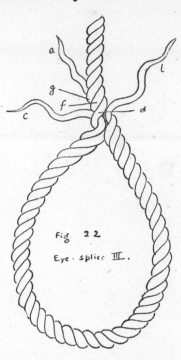

Fig. 22.

Eye-splice III.

Laying in three times is sufficient for everyday eyes. As you pull each end taut, give it a twist to preserve its grip. If you have much trouble with the ends un-laying themselves, "serve" them with twine or any small stuff that is to hand. But they will usually go well enough through the openings if you just double the point.

If you want the splice to be tapered in the most approved style, gradually reduce the ends after each laying in, by cutting away part of the yarns. After this you will, of course, serve and parcel the splice. But as this book is only concerned with such operations as, say, the hirer of a small yacht may be expected to perform, we will leave "worming and parcelling" to be described by a rigger's text-book. Still, the humblest boat-sailor finds it useful to know how to serve the end of a rope to prevent its unlaying itself.

(*e*) *To "serve" an "end."*—Always have by you a small ball of fine tarred twine for

Fig. 23
serving. I

this and the like purposes. Hold the end in your left hand pointing towards your right. Lay the end of the twine along the rope as in Fig. 23. Pass the ball over the rope and round, thus going "against the lay of the rope," which will cause your service to grip the tighter. Catch in the end of the twine and take three or four turns firmly. Pull the end of the twine so as to bring the bight *a* close up to the other turns.

Unroll some of your ball, make a fairly large bight (Fig. 24, *c*), and lay what will

be the other end of your service along the
rope towards the left (Fig. 24). Continue
lapping the twine from *b*, pulling taut,
for four or five more turns, passing the
bight *c* over the end of the rope at each
turn.

Finally, pull the remaining bight (Fig. 25, *e*)
taut, by hauling on the ball end of the twine.
Cut off the ends of the twine quite close;
lay the end of the rope on a board and cut
off square with a sharp knife—a sailor always
has a sharp knife—about $\frac{1}{4}$ inch from the
service.

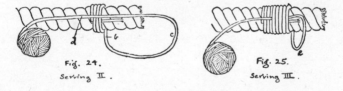

Fig. 24.
Serving II.

Fig. 25.
Serving III.

If, for any reason, you cannot turn the
bight (Fig. 24, *c*) over the end of the rope,
don't form the bight at all. Continue the
turns from *b* over a pricker or a pencil laid
along the rope. Cut off the ball, pass the
end of the twine through the turns, between
the pricker and the rope, withdraw the pricker,
draw the turns taut one by one, beginning

at *b*, and haul the remaining bight taut as before. You will be reduced to this method in lapping the rings on a fishing rod or mending a driving whip, and in many jobs afloat.

CHAPTER VIII

ON SHIP-KEEPING.

NOTHING looks nicer than the white deck of a well-kept ship. But the keeping of such a deck involves daily labour and hourly vigilance. To keep a deck, as it can be kept at sea, becomes an impossibility in a tiny little craft, that is forever mooring alongside a dirty bank, having a muddy quant hastily cast down at odd times in her waterways, and washing-up after every meal performed on her counter. The decks of most small craft in Norfolk are covered with linoleum. Let us resign, therefore, the bucket, the twiddler, the squeegee, the slice of lemon and the oxalic acid to the salt sea sailor, and lay hold upon the mop.

If your boat is a hired one—I have written this book in the hope of alleviating some of the discomforts of those who hire small yachts

—you may find the brown linoleum on your counter black with grease from the washing-up. Powder it all over with a famous powder called Vim and scrub it with a brush. All will be right in ten minutes or so, and you can easily keep it so thenceforward. All you have to do is to swab the entire deck every morning—while breakfast is cooking, say, or while you are under way before breakfast— and swab the counter *after every washing-up.* If you have a really seamanly instinct, you will get all ropes up out of the way and start swabbing on the port quarter, going round the ship the way of the sun (in the northern hemisphere, that is) ; forward to the ship's head along the port side and aft down the starboard side. Go over all the woodwork, inside the well too, in the same way with a wet cloth. Coil down all ropes again and log off for breakfast.

After breakfast you will wash up *before anything else is done.* To postpone washing up, for whatever reason, is a high crime and misdemeanour, with a not to be evaded penalty. After wash-up, swab the counter. Then take dust-pan and brush and remove every single bit of dust, crumb, hair, fluff, etc., from the bunks, the cabin-floor, and the well, and heave it overboard. *Mind that no crumbs find their way below into the bilge.* This must be done after *every* meal, without fail. It makes all the difference and does not take a minute.

But it will take more than a minute if the bunks have not been properly stowed. I assume that, when you turned out, you shook and folded all your blankets neatly, and your pyjamas, and stowed them; that your toilet tackle had been replaced in the little shelf allotted it, and that no purposeless hamper was left lying about; in fact that the necessary law—"a place for everything and everything in its place" — had been rigidly obeyed or enforced — with a rope's end, if necessary.

All these things having been duly carried out, you should be ready to make sail within half an hour from the time you finished breakfast. If they have not been carried out, you will have a less pleasant time than you might have had, and a better one than you deserve.

After the ship is under way, you — or your crew, for I assume you are not sailing alone — will go over all the woodwork of the ship with a leather, to remove every water spot. This, again, takes very little time if it is done every day, but is irksome if postponed.

Take your bottle of metal polish and your polishing cloth from their appointed place and polish every bit of copper and brass till it shines again; still going round the way of the sun. Again a small matter if done daily. The quickest way is to go round twice, once to rub with the polish, once to polish it up after the polish has dried. Replace the tools where they should be.

"Wood - work and brass - work" being finished, you may call "spell-oh," rig up a pipe and remark that "this is a long ship." The satisfaction of having your ship really clean, like the satisfaction of being well dressed, confers a spiritual calm "beyond the power even of religion to bestow."

Ropes, by the way, should be coiled down right-handed, the way of the sun. You will easily acquire the knack of giving each part of the coil the little twist with the hand which causes it to lie obediently in its place. If a coil is going to lie undisturbed for any length of time—say the fall of the forestay tackle—place the end in the centre of the circle and work it round the way of the sun, drawing the rest of the coil round it in a gradually widening spiral. This takes no time, and the result is a very pretty and remarkably durable little mat.

Once a week at least you should find an opportunity—after deck swabbing is best—to go over your "topsides," the outer part of the yacht which is above the water, with mop and leather. You will have to use the dinghy. While you are doing this take a look at the scuppers to see they are not choked with dirt, and clean them out if they are. As you go round, take a look at those parts of the rigging that are not visible from the deck, chain-plates, bobstay, and so forth, to see that they are sound. Disaster often lurks unperceived in such places.

Frequently raise the floor-boards and see how much water there is in the bilge. If it is more than half-way up the floor-timbers, pump or bale it out; otherwise a good list to a squall may shoot some of it into your bunk, and bunks take a long time to get dry.

8

Also it may smell. But the man who does not mind a wet bunk will not bother about details like smells.

Keep an eye to all ropes and cordage. If a rope is badly chafed or stranded, don't wait till it parts, it might cause a deal of damage. Get it repaired or renewed, if you can't put a new strand in it yourself. Don't leave the ends of lacings or points unlaid. They are a nuisance every time you use them, and they look unsailorly. Serve them at once, or on the first occasion when you are looking for a job.

Take the opportunity when the day is fine and you are not under way to air all bedding, rugs, blankets, etc., etc. Everything on the water is more or less damp. Get it and keep it as dry as you can.

Don't get two suits of clothes wet if you can possibly avoid it. A yacht is a small place. Remember the sailor's motto, "the more clothes you have to get wet, the more clothes you have to get dried." Don't immolate your entire wardrobe and think thereby to save yourself trouble.

Never leave your sails stowed wet. As soon as you get a chance, set them; the mainsail with peak lowered and boom topped well up, the jib minus the sheets. Stow again when dry, and put the cover on.

Always, when at anchor, have a mat and a mop to receive the boots of those coming aboard. It saves trouble.

One last piece of advice, in the steward's department. Study how to make your bunk comfortable. The observing sailor will have noticed that when his blankets go on strike they usually seek the floor. They don't try to escape by climbing up the ceiling of the ship's side. If you will well and carefully tuck in that side of your bunk which is next the ceiling, you can leave the other side to take care of itself. It will not try to get adrift on that side. But if it gets adrift the other side there is trouble. So tuck it in well along the outer edge and have a GOOD NIGHT.

CHAPTER IX

THE KITCHEN

THERE seems to be a popular superstition that the sailor in small craft *must* live on tinned tongues, corned beef, sardines and cheese. And it must be admitted that he does so with sufficient frequency to account for the prevalence of this delusion. There are only three tinned foods which I consider it desirable to have on board. 1. Halford's curries. 2. Crosse and Blackwell's tinned beef-steak and kidney puddings and apple puddings. 3. Sardines, herringlets, and the like. And all these are only as " stand-bys," or to be used "for a change." The two first of these carry their own instructions. The third need none.

It is such an addition to the pleasure of a trip to enjoy simple, wholesome meals, and it is so easy to secure them, that I devote this chapter to a few hints, the result of practical experience. And I will endeavour to give these hints in language that will enable " even first - class passengers " to cook their own breakfast.

Utensils.—Firstly, the tools. Two stoves. In large yachts you will find miniature kitchen ranges. I am not concerned with them. I describe a comfortable minimum for a small boat. I have worked with two small tin spirit stoves and much satisfaction, but the fuel bill is alarming. I had rather be shipmates with a " Primus " than any other stove. A man with two " Primus " stoves may do anything but one " Primus " and a small spirit stove will work wonders.

Two or three enamelled saucepans of various sizes.

A double saucepan (for porridge).

A large stew-pan—a most valuable weapon.

A kettle—not an indispensable implement. If you are at all short of room, leave this ashore first.

A fish-slice or egg-lifter, which is also useful in straining the sauce from stews or the water from vegetables.

A tin funnel for filling stoves.

A tin can for paraffin, and another for methylated spirits.

A large jar or " breaker " for fresh water.

Bacon and eggs.—Make the stove burn briskly. Put on the frying-pan and let it get hot. Put the rashers — I assume that you bought your bacon cut in rashers—after removing the outer skin, if necessary, in the pan, but so that they do not lie on top of one another. As soon as the white fat begins to look a bit transparent, turn them over with a fork. When the fat is quite transparent they are done enough to suit most people. Time—for one lot of rashers, about three minutes, if thin ; five minutes if thick. Pile the rashers on a side of the pan where they will not cook any more, but where they will keep hot, and drain. Bacon fries best with very little fat in the pan. Much fat makes it flabby and greasy. In fact, the nearer you can get it to grilling, rather than frying, the better.

But eggs want a fair amount. So, if the bacon has not produced enough, put in a little lard to make enough. Break the eggs. Take a teacup, crack the shell boldly but neatly on the edge of the cup, open the two halves of the shell and let the contents drop into the cup without breaking the yolk. You can break two at a time into the cup, but more than two makes the next operation rather clumsy. Slide them out of the cup into the boiling fat. Let them fry till the white is well set. During the frying all the whites will have joined together. Cut them apart with a sharp knife.

Take out the bacon, keeping it as dry as possible, and lay it on the plates—dishes being a luxurious nuisance in small craft. Lift the eggs with the egg - lifter without breaking them, keeping them as clear of fat as possible, and lay them with the bacon.

Time all told, about twelve minutes.

While you are doing the bacon you will have either water or milk in progress on the second stove for tea or coffee or cocoa. Mind you don't burn the milk or overboil it; it should just be brought to boiling point, but not actually boiled. A good coffee extract with hot milk makes excellent *café au lait*. If you like a certain amount of water in either coffee or cocoa, add the water to the milk and heat them together. The result will be better than coffee or cocoa made with water, and milk added subsequently.

Cooking being over, pour off the fat from the frying - pan into a cup for future use. Put some water into the milk saucepan—river water will do—and boil it up again to make the saucepan clean easily. Fill the wash-bowl with river water — it is a popular but fallacious superstition which asserts that you cannot wash up with cold water — and put into it about a tablespoonful of washing soda, which will melt while you are eating ; and all will be ready for work when you have finished.

Hot plates are a desirable luxury and easily obtainable, if you make porridge. Don't use lids to cover your saucepans. Use plates, which will cover the pan well enough and become hot in doing so. But the milk or the water for breakfast does not boil long enough to heat the plates well. Porridge does. As it is an excellent food, and easy to prepare, begin breakfast with it, and have really hot plates for the subsequent bacon.

Porridge. — Into the outer part of the double saucepan put enough river water to cover well the bottom of the inner part. Into the inner part put as many half-pints of water from the jar as you want porridge. Bring it to the boil.

To each half-pint of water allow 1 oz. to
1¼ oz. of medium Scotch oatmeal of the
very best quality. The very best is inappreci-
ably more costly than mediocre oatmeal, and
the difference in the eating is immense.

As the water is about to boil, sprinkle
the oatmeal into the water, stirring all the
while. If you put the meal in too soon,
you will have a tedious stirring. If the
water is boiling fast, the meal will go into
lumps and give trouble. This is the critical
moment. Keep stirring until the meal swells
or thickens. Left alone, the meal will sink
and coagulate into lumps, so stir continually
at least—continuously is better. If the stove
is doing its duty, thickening will occur in
ten minutes or a little less. You may now
reduce the flame and allow the pot to simmer
for twenty minutes more. During this interval
you may attack other jobs, tidying the cabin
or swabbing decks or completing your toilet.
Then put in the salt, a small teaspoonful to
each half-pint—but tastes differ. Another
ten minutes' simmering, a good stir when you
put the salt in and another when you take
the pot off, and the porridge is ready.

As you seldom have a balance on board,

it is useful to know that a good tablespoonful, not too much heaped, is about an ounce of oatmeal. Try it ashore before you start. Don't cook your porridge overnight. It is best freshly made.

To summarise this most important operation :—

7.10 A.M.	Light stove and put on pot.
7.20 ,,	Put in meal.
7.30 ,,	Meal thickens.
7.50 ,,	Put in salt.
8.0 ,,	Serve.

These times are calculated for a " Primus." A weaker stove may extend them by fifteen minutes.

If you like your bacon hot, don't begin to cook it till you have eaten your porridge. The " crew " may grumble at waiting, but the result will console both them and you.

Fill the inner saucepan with the boiling water from the outer one, to make it clean easily, and stand it aside.

Buttered eggs. — Use an ounce of butter to every two eggs. Break the eggs into a cup and beat up with a little pepper and salt and a fork. Melt the butter in a small saucepan and stir the eggs up with it.   Warm it over a gentle flame and keep stirring till the mixture thickens. Then serve.

Some cooks put milk into this. It "makes more" and spoils the dish.

Mushrooms.—"Mushers" are often procurable in Broadland. (Don't turn up your nose at "horse-mushrooms." Eat them and you will be thankful.) Peel them. The skin comes off easily from the edge towards the middle. Pepper and salt. Fry till tender—about five minutes; but big mushers take longer than little ones.

Chopped up, fried lightly, and mixed with the buttered eggs in cooking, they make an excellent mixture.

Yarmouth, the centre of Broadland, is the home of *herrings.* As fresh herrings and as bloaters they are best grilled. The nearest approach you can make to this is to cook them in the frying-pan, with just enough grease to prevent their sticking to it, and turn them continually. But as kippers, especially in the small form of "longshores," they lend themselves to the resources of our "cooking locker." Put a little water in the frying-pan, an eighth to a quarter of an inch. Butter the red sides of the kippers. When the water boils, lay them in it, skin side down. Five to ten minutes, from the time the water boils *after the kippers were put into it*, will do them nicely. Haddocks can be done the same way.

Boiling. Note.—The time a thing takes to boil is calculated from the time the water begins to boil again after the thing has been put in. Putting a cold thing into boiling water "takes the water off the boil." The time of boiling is reckoned from the moment when the water recovers its boiling property.

Steaks, chops, sausages, etc. — These may all be fried, but, like bacon, with as little fat as possible. They should, of course, be grilled. And if you have a " grill-pan," a thing like a corrugated frying-pan, grill them by all means. But the condition of an oil or spirit stove after an attempt at grilling with a grid is best described in the language of the man who has to clean it.

Stews.—The best thing to do with meat on a small boat is to make a stew ; thus :—

Peel and slice an onion and fry it a nice golden brown. If you like the meat to be brown when stewed, fry that too, but lightly.

Prepare the vegetables. Potatoes and

turnips should be washed and peeled : carrots washed and scraped : beans should have the strings removed.

Slice all the vegetables and put them in the stew-pan with the fried onions and the meat, and enough water just not to cover them. A little salt and pepper.

Bring the whole to a boil, then turn the flame low and let it simmer gently. Stir now and again to prevent it from " catching." About an hour's simmering should do it. Try the ingredients by prodding them with a fork.

The fried part will brown the gravy. The potatoes will thicken it. But should it not be thick enough, do this :—

Mix a little cornflour with *cold* water in a teacup. Take the meat and vegetables out of the pan with the egg-lifter and lay them in a hot dish (which, with the plates, should have been standing on top of the stew-pan while cooking was in progress). Mix some of your cornflour paste with the gravy, warming it and adding paste till it is thick enough. Pour over the meat and vegetables in the dish, and serve.

Put some river water in the stew-pan and

set it back on the stove to boil and make
it clean easily.

Vegetables. — Potatoes, well scrubbed and
boiled in their skins, are excellent. If you
peel them, do it in cold water. New potatoes
need only be scraped in cold water. Very
new potatoes should only be scrubbed. But
old potatoes boiled "in their jackets" are
perhaps best of all.

To boil. — Allow half a tablespoonful of salt
to a quart of water. Choose potatoes about
of a size, because the larger ones take longer
to cook. Old potatoes should be put into the
water when cold; new potatoes when it boils.
From twenty to thirty minutes' boiling will
cook them. Small new potatoes may only
take fifteen minutes. (*See note on boiling
above.*)

Potatoes are also excellent sliced and fried.
They want plenty of fat, and they take
some time and care, because they must be
done one layer at a time and not in a
heap. When you see the edges going brown
and the white transparent turn them over
and brown the other side. When they are
soft inside (try them with a fork), lay them
on a cool part of the pan, just to keep

warm and drain, and proceed with another layer.

You may use up old cold potatoes this way to advantage.

The preparation of cabbages, brussels sprouts and the like involves more space and time than small craft can afford. They are not handy things. If you must have them, remember these points. After stripping off the outer leaves and cutting off the stalks, soak them well in salt and water for some time, half an hour say. Don't put them into the saucepan till the water boils well. Don't put the lid or any cover on the saucepan, or their colour will be wrong.

But *beans*, French and Runner, are just the thing. Nip off the tops and tails and pull out the strings from back and front. If the beans are young and nicely grown—size is nothing to go by—there will be no strings. If the strings are very strong and the beans hard, put them overside. You won't like them and the cooking will be a waste of time. Who bought them?

Slice them and boil in salted water for about fifteen minutes. Drain off the water—with the help of the egg-lifter—and get them as dry as possible. Put a little butter on them in the hot dish and toss them about with a fork to distribute the butter equitably.

If the beans are very young they are better cooked whole, not sliced, and buttered as above. The flavour is not in the least like that of sliced beans. They are said, too, to be much more nutritious cooked whole than sliced.

Rice.—I have already mentioned Halford's Curries as a good standby. But curry without rice is unthinkable, and it is easy to do rice. Wash the rice in cold water to remove the rice flour, which would tend to stick the grains together. Sprinkle the rice into water that is boiling *fast*, stirring the while. Sprinkle it in little by little so as not to stop the boiling. Let the water be about three times the quantity of rice by measure. Let it boil as fast as possible—" gallop," as the cook says. In about ten minutes add a little salt. In fifteen to twenty minutes it should be done. Try a grain by rubbing it between the forefinger and thumb. It should rub all away. When it is done, take off the saucepan and throw into it a little cold water to check the boiling instantly. This will cause the grains to separate. Strain off the water. Hold the saucepan again over the flame and toss the rice with a fork, to get it hot and dry. When it looks nice and white and every grain separate but soft, serve.

Devil.—In Broadland one can often buy a cold cooked fowl or duck from a farmhouse. Drumsticks and the like remains make a better dish devilled than cold.

For devil, mix up in a cup with a knife half an ounce of butter, half a teaspoonful each of mustard, salt, and black pepper, and a good pinch of Cayenne or Nepaul. Slit the meat and insert this mixture. Heat well in the frying-pan, and serve.

Sausages are very good devilled in this way.

Eels.—If you are afraid of the eels having a muddy flavour, soak them for a night in strong brine after skinning and cleaning them. But if you want them for supper, you will not be able to keep them in brine during the day while you are sailing.

The best way to skin an eel is to put a fork through the back of his neck (and push it well into the ground if you are ashore). Slit the skin round his neck behind the fork

9

with a very sharp knife. With the point of the knife push the upper part of the skin back until you can get a good hold with the edge of the knife. Then take hold and pull. The skin will come off backwards inside out. The only difficulty is to get it to start. You will, of course, have previously slit the eel open and cleaned him well. A swab will give you a good grip of him. The bare hand has not a chance.

Eels, says Tom Ingoldsby, should be "spatchcocked or stewed. They're too oily if fried"; and I agree. Most of the cookery books will give you wondrous instructions for stewing eels, with wine sauces and unimagined luxuries, equally unnecessary and impossible for the simple sailor man. Stew them his way and you will be satisfied. Cut them into two- or three-inch lengths and put them in a saucepan or stew-pan with a little salt, a little bit of butter, and water enough just not to cover them. Bring them to the boil, and then simmer gently twenty minutes to half an hour. At the end of that time, unless they are very large, the flesh will leave the bones easily, and they are done.

Some put fine breadcrumbs, white, into

the gravy and so make a thick white sauce, which is not to be despised.

Others, having taken out the eels before they were quite done, put them into the frying-pan and finish the operation by frying them a nice brown.

I have written thus much about eels because they are a dish readily and cheaply procurable on the Broads, and very welcome to most people.

With the assistance of the above hints a beginner can make himself comfortably independent of corned beef and the like tinned abominations. But the cleanliness of the utensils is a necessary condition of success, which brings us to *washing - up*. A few general hints should suffice.

Every vessel after cooking should be filled with water—river water will usually do—and replaced on the stove to boil. If the ordinary soda and water will not clean it thoroughly, a little " Vim " will soon bring it to reason ; or use a " Lian " pot-scrubber, a god-send to scullery-maids. Rinse it well in the river after washing, and stand it upside down to drain.

As before advised (p. 98), you will have

filled your wash-bowl with water and put some
soda in it. Have a swab ready in the bowl.
Have some newspaper torn into convenient
squares. Have two cloths ready, one for
drying, one for polishing.

Rub "the worst" off the plates, etc., with
paper, which you will throw overboard.
(Having "an overboard" is one of the
advantages of life afloat.) Then scrub the
plates *quite clean* with the swab, both sides,
giving each one a good rinse in the river
after washing. Do the same with the knives
and forks. The "crew" should "stand by"
with the drying and polishing cloths to complete your work. If, after a day or two,
you find your drying cloth becoming greasy,
the washing has not been done thoroughly,
and the washer requires to be severely
reprimanded.

Wash the plates, knives, forks, etc., *one by
one*. *Never* put them into the wash-bowl all
together, as is the custom of shore folk. If
you do, sooner or later you will throw something overboard. It is more difficult to
recover a spoon from the mud of the river-
bed than to extract it from a sink pipe.

Well rinse and wring out the swab. Well

rinse and clean the wash-bowl. Hang out the swab and the two cloths to dry (W.P.), swab the counter with the mop perfectly clean (I assume that you have used the counter to wash up on), light your pipe and enjoy the repose of the just.

EDITOR'S NOTE : All the above was, of course, written before rationing and many of the food items mentioned are not currently or easily available. Nevertheless, the advice is sound and will suffice when food is again freely available.

CHAPTER X

Belaying Pin.

the Muck Fleet, War Fleet (Dartmouth), Fleet
Street (E.C.), etc.

Flemish knot, 71.

Flukes. The hooking part of an anchor. Pronounced
"flues."

Fore and aft. In the direction of the ship's keel.
At right angles to athwartships. Fore and aft
sails are contrasted with "square," which are set
athwartships.

Foredeck, v. Parts of a ship, 121.

Forepeak, v. Parts of a ship, 121.

Forestay, v. Parts of a ship, 121.

Forward. Towards the ship's head. Opposite of aft.
Pronounced "forrad."

Frap. To bind round. St Paul's sailors frapped their
ship.

Full and by. With sails full though by, *i.e.* close
to, the wind.

Gaff, v. Parts of a ship, 121. Warnings *re,* 30, 51.

Get. To "get" an anchor is to get it on board.

Getting under way. Chapter II. The key of the
difficulty, 21.

Girt. A wrinkle.

Gooseneck. The universal joint of the boom.

Granny, 75.

Greens, to cook, **105.**

Gunwale. The timber which is fitted on top of the
frames or ribs to which the top strake is fastened.
Pronounced "gunnel." (Inwale, a similar timber
in small boats, has a sounded *w.* About the
only sea-going word that has.)

Gybe. With the wind abaft the beam a ship is
said to be on port or starboard gybe. *Cf.* Tack.

When she changes from one gybe to the other she is said to gybe, or you are said to gybe her.

Hail. To call. "Within easy hail" = at such a distance that a message may easily be shouted, or a signal easily seen.

Halyards. Ropes for hauling up the sails. Warning *re*, 59.

Hand-taut. As taut as a straight pull can make it.

Haul. To pull. For "haul down" and "haul aft" *v.* Sheets.

Hawser, v. Yarn.

Head. (i.) The forward ond of a ship. (ii.) *v.* Parts of a sail, 120.

Helm. The tiller. Its positions are described as aport, amidships, astarboard; hard aport and hard astarboard (either being called hard over) being the extremes : also as "up," *i.e.*, to windward, and "down," to leeward; hard up and hard down. As a ship usually tends towards the wind, the helm has to be kept up to keep her on her course. She is then said to "carry weather-helm." If the opposite is the case, she "carries lee-helm"—very undesirable. To "ease the helm" is to relax the pressure of weather-helm, which allows the ship to come to the wind. When a ship is going about her helm is put "alee," the helmsman calling "helm's alee" or "lee-oh" to warn the crew.

Herrings, to cook, 101.

Hot-plates, to secure, 98.

Housing. The part of the mast below the deck.

Jib, to set, 10 ; to lower, 57 ; to stow, 61.

Jibboom. An extension of the bowsprit in large vessels.

Kippers, 101.

Knot. (i.) In rope, Chapter VII. (ii.) A measure of distance, a nautical mile; which is a minute of latitude measured on a meridian. Not the same thing as a geographical mile, which is a minute of longitude measured along the equator. A knot has no fixed dimension; it varies in actual length from 6046 feet about the equator to 6109 feet at the poles. Its "mean" is usually taken as 6080 feet.

Lay. A rope is "laid," the strands being twisted together to keep them laid. The lay is the direction in which the strands are laid up together.

Lead, pronounced "led," is the sounding apparatus.

Lead, pronounced "leed," is the direction of a rope. When a rope passes directly to its passage through a block or a bull's-eye, without let or hindrance or crossing any other rope, the lead is said to be fair. Otherwise it is foul. Holes in coamings and bulls'-eyes are also spoken of as leads or fair-leads.

Lee, Leeward. The direction towards which the wind is blowing. Opposite of windward. Pronounced "looard," "windard."

By the lee, 24; alee, *v.* Helm.

Leeway. In sailing by or on a wind a boat is driven a little to leeward. This aberration from her course is called leeway, and is defined as the angle which the vessel's keel makes with her wake. It does not much concern sailors on inland waters.

Lie. When a ship can hold on a course without shaking her sails she is said to be able to lie the course.

Luff. (i.) *v.* Parts of a sail ; (ii.) a verb, to luff; to let the ship's head come to the wind.

Mainsail, to set, 8 ; to lower, 57 ; to stow, 58.

Main-sheet, v. Parts of a ship, 121 ; and *v.* Sheet. Warnings *re* main-sheet, 9, 42, 43.

Marline-spike. A pointed weapon of wood or metal for opening the strands of a rope.

Marline - spike.

Mast, to lower, 66 ; to raise 68.

Mast - hoops. The hoops that keep the luff of the mainsail up to the mast.

Meeting end on, 45 and 49.

Milk, hints on boiling, 97.

Moor. To make a ship fast so that she will not move from her position. A ship at anchor swings with wind or tide the whole distance permitted by the amount of cable she has out. Moored with two anchors, she rides first to one and then to the other, and cannot move far. Moored fore and aft to a quay or the rond she cannot move at all, *v.* Chapter VI. p. 61, *et sqq.*

Mushrooms, 101.

Muzzle, 57.

Narrow waters, advantage of learning in, 1.

Night, prevention of noises at; halyards, 61 ; lapping water, 54 ; dinghy, 64.

Outhaul. A rope for hauling the corner of a sail or other object out to the end of a spar.

Overhand knot, 71.

Overhaul. To haul on the standing part of a rope that passes through blocks so as to increase the distance between the blocks. This is at times necessary, especially if the rope does not render freely.

Overtaking, 47 and 49.

Parcel. To cover with canvas.

Parrel or Parral, 67.

Parts of a sail, v. Diagram.

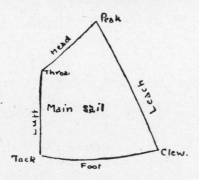
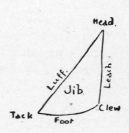

Parts of a ship, v. Diagram, 121.

Pay off, 17.

Peak, v. Parts of a sail.

Peak halyard. The halyard which hoists the peak.

Porridge, 99.

Port. The left hand side, looking forward.

Port gybe. Off or before a wind blowing from the port hand. Chapter III. p. 23.

Port tack. By or on a wind blowing from the port hand. Chapter V. p. 45.

Potatoes, to boil, or to fry, 104.

Pricker. A small marline-spike.

Purchase. An arrangement of blocks to obtain extra power.

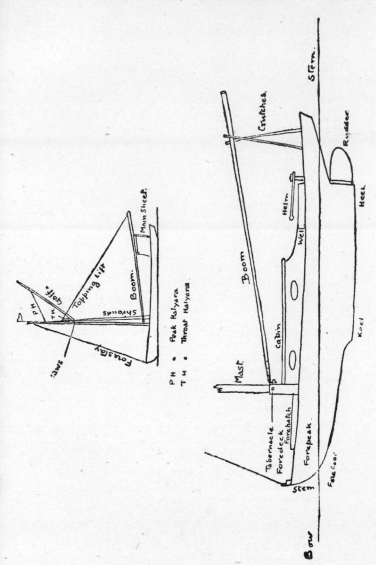

Quant. A punt pole. Its peculiarity is a foot bolted to one side of the point, which prevents its going too deeply into mud and enables the quanter to extract it easily by giving it a twist, which, using the foot as a fulcrum, breaks out the point. A very ancient word. In "The Abbot," the boat in which Mary escapes from Lochleven Castle is shoved as far as may be with a "kent," oars being too noisy. Charon shoved his "cerulean wherry" across the Styx with a quant, *conto, Æneid* vi. The same word occurs in Greek.

Quarter. The after part of a ship.

Quiff. A tweak, wrinkle or ingenious device.

Reaching, 22.

Reef knot, 74.

Reefing, 38.

Reeve. To thread like a needle. You reeve a rope through a block or a bull's-eye. Its past participle is rove.

Rice, to boil, 106.

Roger. A special brand of squall, brewed in Norfolk.

Rond Anchor

Rolling bend, 79.

Rond. The bank. Also spelt Raund. Dutch Rand.

Rond anchor. A stockless anchor with one fluke used for anchoring by the rond.

Rope, v. Yarn. Is measured by circumference. Parts of a rope, *v.* Chapter VII. p. 72.

Rule of the Road. Chapter V.

Running, 23.

Stop. To tie up with yarn or twine.

Strake. A boat is planked with strakes (streaks).

Strand. The parts which are twisted up to form a rope are strands, *v.* Yarn. If one strand gives way, the rope is said to be stranded.

Stretch off the land = Taking a caulk = forty winks or shut-eye. When a vessel is beating, say in the Channel, and goes about to make her next reach across, she will meet with no danger for some hours : a favourable opportunity of which the "old man" avails himself. Hence the expression. For "taking a caulk," *cf.* Danish and Swedish, "going to listen to the leak."

Strop. A ring of rope or metal. (Strap.)

Swig. To pull on a rope at right angles to it, both ends being fast, so as to get extra power on it.

Swinging her round, 19.

Tabernacle, 66.

Tack. (i.) *See* Parts of a sail, 120. (ii.) A board to windward ; port tack with the wind on your port hand and starboard the opposite. If the wind is abaft the beam, you are, properly speaking, not on a tack but on a gybe, though the word is used to cover this case also.

Tackle. A purchase. Pronounced "taykle."

Taunt. Tall. A taunt ship is one having long masts ; contrasted with "square," *i.e.,* having long yards. The expression "a long ship" indicates that the speaker is thirsty. Why ?

Taut. Tight.

Thimble. The metal fitting for the inside of an eye.

Tholes. Pins to row against.

Throat, v. Parts of a sail, **120.**

Throat halyard. The halyard that hoists the throat.

Thwarts. Seats of an open boat. They serve, as the deck beams of a yacht, to stiffen the boat. Pronounce, "thoughts." Hence athwart = across; and athwartships = at right angles to the keel.

Tinned meats, 94.

Topping-lift. The rope that "tops" the boom, *v.* Parts of a ship, 121; warnings *re,* 9, 40, 59.

Topsides, 91.

Tow, the. Means the vessel being towed.

Traveller. An iron or metal ring travelling on a spar.

Trim. (i.) Of sails, to give the necessary amount of sheet. (ii.) Of ballast, to arrange it so that the boat lies "on an even keel," both fore and aft and athwartships. The latter should properly be called on an even bilge.

Two-blocks, v. Block.

Tyers. Pieces of rope, sennit, or canvas to tie up furled sails.

Unlay. To untwist a rope, *v.* Lay.

Unship, v. Ship.

Up-helm, v. Helm.

Up-mast, 68.

Vegetables, to cook, 104.

Wake. The track left by a ship.

Warnings, re anchoring, 20, 63, 64; boom when running, 26; chainplates, 91; coils projecting, 12; dinghy, 15, 64; gaff, 30, 51; gybing, 24; halyards, 59; main-sheet, 39, 42, 43; peak halyard, 8; reef-points, 37, 40; sheets, 13, 42, 43; shelving bottom, 62; stowing anchors, etc., 14; topping-lift, 9, 40, 59; washing-up, 88, 110.

Warp. Rope for hauling a boat about, making fast to piers, etc.

Washing-up, 109.

Way. The movement of a ship through the water; whence also lee-way, steerage-way, stern-way. Sometimes spelt "weigh," wrongly, though there is a distant philological connection between the words.

Way, getting under. Chapter II.

Weather. Adjective = windward; whence aweather; also the weather shore and your weather eye.

Weather-helm, v. Helm.

Weigh. To raise (its original meaning).

Well. The open part of a partially decked boat. When a well is very small and water-tight it is called a cock-pit.

Wherry. In Norfolk a large shallow barge of 40-60 tons, carrying one huge gaff sail with no boom. Under an able sailor wherries are capable of very neat handling. Though an old wherryman told me that "it takes two clever men to understand one of them things."

Wind aft. Rule of the road and directions, 46, 52.

Windward. The direction from which the wind is blowing; opposite of leeward, *q.v.*

Worm, to. To fill up the spaces between the strands of a rope with twine, preparatory to serving and parcelling.

Yarn. (i.) The strands of a rope are made of twisted yarns. Three or four strands are twisted up to form a rope or hawser. Hawsers twisted up form a cable. Four-stranded rope is laid up round a "heart" or core; otherwise the rope would be

hollow and the strands would pull out of place ;
(ii.) A story.   A tall story is a tough yarn, and
should it contain a point of such magnitude as to
require a heavy purchase to hoist it in, it becomes
a bender.

Yaw.   Of the vessel, to go this way and that, instead
of holding a steady course.   Of the steersman, to
cause her to do so.

SAILING RULES.

Dont's and Hints for the Novice.

Note:—These have been extracted from Blake's Ltd. Yearly List and included to assist novices.

Owing to the Rivers of Norfolk and Suffolk being narrow in places it is essential those in charge of craft be well acquainted with the " Rule of the Road," especially the novice. The following chief rules and hints, we hope, will be carefully noted :—

Looking forward from the well of the yacht, the port side is the left and the right is the starboard side. Windward, the side from which the wind is blowing. Leeward, the opposite side.

A yacht is on the port tack when the sails are over the starboard side, and on the starboard tack when they are over the port side.

1. A vessel which is close-hauled on the port tack shall keep out of the way of a vessel which is close-hauled on the starboard tack.

2. When both are running free, with the wind on different sides, the vessel which has the wind on the port side shall keep out of the way of the other. This often occurs on the Broads if you have a beam wind and meet another boat coming towards you.

3. A yacht running free keeps out of the way of one close-hauled.

4. A yacht overtaking another must keep out of the way of the overtaken yacht.

Don't forget a wherry's gaff sticks out a long way, so keep to windward if possible.

Don't refuse kindly advice—it is offered in the right spirit.

Don't pinch your yacht when tacking ; keep her sails full, and way on her. Even if you are not gaining much you will make it up on the turn.

Don't try and moor on the lee bank with all your sails full ; you are likely to have a nasty accident. If you cannot find room on the windward bank lower away, even if you have to quant to your moorings. Always bring your boat head to wind when mooring.

Don't forget to treat a hired yacht as though it was your own : keep it clean, spick and span, and everything nice and shipshape— it helps things to run smoothly.

Don't sail with a taut topping lift, badly set sails, or leave your fenders hanging overboard. These denote the novice.

Don't forget to tighten up your topping lift before you lower your sails when moored. It holds the boom, and nasty accidents can be prevented this way. Slack away, however, after you have got your sail-cover on and boom in crutches, as if it rains it is surprising how this takes up.

Don't be offended if some good soul points out these defects, but thank him and correct at once.

Don't have your dinghy yards behind ; a foot is quite enough, and keeps it handy and not in the way of other craft.

Don't think the land to which you moor is a dumping-ground for your odds and ends of papers, etc. Just keep them all together and burn same, and leave the place tidy, and thus show your consideration for the Owners.

Don't forget if other people are moored near you they are on holiday and want rest about the usual bed-time. If you feel you must make a noise, just move your boat up or down the river, as there is plenty of room for you out of hearing.

Don't cover up your sails if wet, but stow very loosely, and get same dry by hoisting at first opportunity Many sails are spoilt this way, owing to mildew setting in.

Don't be in a hurry to get off. Take your time and see that everything is O.K. If another yacht is coming, let her pass.

Don't forget although motor craft give way to sailing craft there are exceptions, and it is best for you to keep clear than have an accident.

Don't forget to learn how to reef properly, as a torn sail is a costly item.

Don't forget to take off the gaff before you lower the mast.

Don't forget you can't steer a boat unless you have way on her independent of the tide.

Don't sail with your cabin-top up.

Don't leave your quant behind.

Don't take the mast and sail of the dinghy unless you really mean to use them often. They are always in the way. If you take them, see the mast does not protrude over the bows when towing.

Don't forget to be very careful when you are sailing with a heavy wind right aft, as a gybe will no doubt occur and wants careful handling.

Don't stand on the sails, as the marks are difficult to get out.

Don't forget to read how to work a Primus stove.

Don't forget although you may be sailing you should understand motor and steam vessel signals.

MOTOR and STEAM VESSEL SIGNALS and OTHER HINTS.

The person in charge of steam or craft under power should signal as follows :—

One short blast, meaning, " I am directing my course to starboard."

Two short blasts : " I am directing my course to port."

Three short blasts : " I am going full speed astern."

Motor boats usually pass each other port to port.

When passing several racing craft being towed from one Regatta to another, please slow up : they are very difficult to manage and the wash knocks them about ; it also causes them to ship water.

Also slow up when passing moored craft. Perhaps the Primus is going, and it is not pleasant to have a kettle of boiling water upset or one's meal spoilt.

HOW TO RUN MOTOR CRUISERS
ON THE NORFOLK BROADS

By EXPERT

This little article takes the form of an imaginary conversation between the Hirer and the Owner. It gives his reception at the boat-yard and the hints given during a trial run.

GOOD AFTERNOON, GENTLEMEN, glorious day to start a holiday ! May this weather continue all through your trip. Yes, that's your ship, and as she

Arrival is quite ready and clean inside, you can get on board and make yourselves at home by unpacking and stowing your gear away, and changing into river clothes and shoes. By that time your fuel and fresh water will be on board. Your stores ? Yes, here they are, and when you are ready I will give you a lift aboard with them.

Stores and Gear Trunks ? Yes, leave them in this shed when you have unpacked, they take up a lot of room on board. Well, just you give me a call when you are ready to start and I will come along and explain the various items.

Ready gentlemen ? Right ! First thing is, have you

been down on the Broads before ? No ! well probably you will have a fine trouble-free holiday ; this craft is as fool-proof as we can supply to date, but we do get a few parties who I fear think they know more than I do about the job, in fact they listen to all I say with an entire disregard for the fact they are shortly to take on the handling of £500 worth of boat, in fact they are out for a good time and hang the consequences. No, gentlemen, I can see you are not like that, so if you can spare ten minutes or so, I will do what I can to put you right.

Experience

Have you found everything you want ? Yes, you cook in that compartment, and although the risk of fire is not very great you should remember you are very near a petrol motor in a confined space, and care should be taken in extinguishing matches and controlling your stove. Now about the motor ; and in connection with this important item, I would like one of you gentlemen to make himself responsible for its operation, and take particular note of its needs ; firstly, lubrication. Here is the oil filler hole, the level is right at the moment but will lower as engine is used ; pour in sufficient each day to bring this float to correct height. Some engines have a dip rod which must be removed, wiped and then inserted and inspected to see if oil is up to level marked.

Fire

Engine

Lubrication

Use good oil. Here is a greaser on water pump and on stern tube bearing, keep these well filled and screwed down each day. The lubrication is carried

Grease : Lubri- cating System

out by a small constantly-working pump, which fills troughs in crankcase from sump and is shown to be working by any pressure this gauge shows. If pressure

Caution gauge shows zero stop your motor or it will seize up. Your engine is water-cooled, and pumps water from the river through engine and out by way of exhaust. Take a look at times and see this water is being ejected ; if

Water Circulation it stops flowing, your intake under the bottom is fouled with weeds, and a good plan is to stop the motor whilst the boat is going ahead. This may clear it and you can start motor again. If it is not cleared, stop boat alongside bank and pass the mop along bottom in way of intake to remove weeds.

Electric light ? Yes, that's mechanically charged by motor, but it is as well to realize you are not on the

Electric Light mains, so switch off when not in use. You should have very little trouble in starting motor. Turn on petrol, lift needle of carburettor to flood it, set throttle lever nearly closed, then pull engine over a few times with

Starting Motor switch off. Then switch on and give a pull up and she should go. Let her run easily for a bit to warm up, and we shall be ready for a trial run. Thanks for bringing

Getting Under Way the anchors on board, it's a good plan to stow them carefully, together with the ropes, as a trailing rope is not only very unyachtsmanlike, but a danger as it may foul the propeller. What does the oil gauge show ? Two pounds ! Good ! and water coming from

Oil and Water

exhaust, splendid. Always see these are working before you start away. Now will the gentleman who is going to steer please take the helm, and then we will go ahead.

Steering
Right Speed

We can now give her some more speed up to three-quarter throttle, which is the best speed to run. Your boat is going comfortably and almost as fast as at full throttle and far more economically.

Close your throttle a good bit, sir, as we are going through that bridge, and be ready to go astern which is by pulling your lever right back.

Shooting Bridges
Going Astern

Give a few toots on the horn : right ! Now here are a lot of boats at their moorings, so go a bit steady past them, as a rocking boat loses much paint against a quay side. Now we are clear and can resume our three-quarter throttle again. By the way, sir, keep generally to the right-hand side of the river, and of course, always pass other power craft on the right side. If you meet a sailing boat coming towards you, hugging the bank, she is no doubt sailing close to the wind, therefore you should give way and go outside her. Do not wait till she is nearly on you before you show your intentions.

Your Course

What about that sailing boat ? Yes, that's another problem. They have the right of way as they have to make use of the wind only to progress.

Passing Sailing
Craft

That chap is tacking, that is, he is going from side to side in progressive steps to get against the wind. You

had better close your throttle, the motor won't stop as it
has slow-running adjustment. Keep well over the
right side, and hold your boat up until you are just
behind him as he starts to tack over the other side.
Then go ahead quickly, and you will be out of his way
before he comes over again. Good! I know it's
tantalising to wait, but remember you are both on
holiday, and not having a race. Never go across the
bows of a boat tacking.

Here's an opening to a Broad just here, so as we are
going in just ease her and sound the horn; splendid
these Broads, aren't they, and now
Broad Entrances we are on here just try turning her
round as sharp as she will go. Good!
she will turn round in the river almost anywhere. Now
see how quickly you can pull her up. Close your
throttle a bit and pull lever right back, now open your
throttle again. You may need that
Practice Whilst operation in an emergency so do it a
In Open Water few times. Remember: always ease
your throttle before changing from
ahead to astern or vice versa. Now we are in the river
again and she seems to be labouring a bit. I think we
have some weeds on the propeller, and you can pick up
a lot of those on your cruise, especially
Weeds on on weedy Broads. Ease throttle again,
Propeller and go into reverse for a few seconds,
then ahead, then astern, for a few
alternate times, this will usually unwind them. Yes!
there they are astern. If this operation won't do the
trick, lay alongside the bank with motor stopped and
pull them off with the boathook. Now, if you think

you have gone far enough with me, turn the boat round and make for the starting place. Keep throttle just open and make for right hand side of

Turning   river, not *too* close. Now put your helm hard over and hold it there. That stops the boat and she will pivot round ; just done it ? Good ! Now clear any possible weeds again, as you usually pick them up when turning. On our way back a few tips might help you. Your motor is a good one, and should not stop invol-

Reliability   untarily except for dirty plugs (which you can easily remove and clean) and dirty fuel supply or water in it, and you will know this by difficult starting and uneven running. To clean this, remove the two caps from under carburettor and then with key in tool locker unscrew jets, clean out and replace *exactly* as before. Don't please tinker

Don't Tinker   with the motor as you can't improve it. If you get any trouble which cannot be rectified without taking any part of the motor down, don't do it ! Telephone me (the owner) from the nearest post office, and I will see your delay is as short as possible. Remember it's my business to see you have a good holiday, but I bar dirty plugs, blocked carburettors, and weedy propellers. You must see to these. Legally you are entirely responsible for boat and engine when I have left you. Now, sir !

Who is in   You are in control at the moment,
Control   and I wish you to make certain, any of your party who will wish to handle the boat out at any time, are as familiar with the operation as you are, and this I leave to you, otherwise it's equal to a motor bus driver letting a passenger steer a

Yarmouth

little way. I presume you are going through Yarmouth, so I advise you to get there when the rather strong tide is slack, the local papers will give you the time, also tide table in " Norfolk Broads Holidays Afloat." Your reserve of power is not great, so try not to put yourself in the position of wanting more than your motor will do.

Now, gentlemen, no travelling after dark. You have no navigating lights, and the owner refrains from supplying them for that reason. Not only is

**No Travelling
After Dark**

it unnecessary, but extremely foolish and a grave danger to other craft. Not only is this so, but such action on your part is against the bye-laws, and you are open to prosecution. Now to other matters. Please keep

Fendoffs

fendoffs from trailing in the water, it spoils them, and it is very bad form. Keep your dinghy fairly close up to stern, and don't jump into it from the boat when going

Dinghy

along, as it's a dangerous practice. When mooring against quays, put your fendoffs so as to take the chafe, but don't use fendoffs at a grassy bank, as the boat's side will wash and fendoffs won't. When arriving at a

Mooring.

mooring, it is best to stop against the tide. It helps you to ease her up a bit.

Well, that's about all, and I expect you think, a good job too. But remember, I want you to have a holiday

free from trouble and accident, and
Cleanliness   moreover, someone else will want their
holiday on this boat when you return,
so do your best to keep the whole job in a spick and span
condition. Well are you ready ? You have sufficient
oil and grease for the motor for your trip and everything
is O.K. Remember, not later than
Time of Return   10 a.m. on the Saturday you return, as
I have to get the boat ready for the
next party, who will expect and are entitled to the same
readiness and attention you have received. Good luck,
gentlemen,   Off you go !